AEPS™

Assessment, Evaluation,
and Programming System
for Infants and Children

SECOND EDITION

VOLUME 2 Test

Birth to Three Years
and Three to Six Years

D1384955

Other volumes in the AEPS series
edited by Diane Bricker, Ph.D.

AEPS Administration Guide

by Diane Bricker, Ph.D., Kristie Pretti-Frontczak, Ph.D.,
JoAnn (JJ) Johnson, Ph.D., and Elizabeth Straka, Ph.D., CCC-SLP,
with Betty Capt, Ph.D., OTR, Kristine Slentz, Ph.D.,
and Misti Waddell, M.S.

AEPS Curriculum for
Birth to Three Years

by Diane Bricker, Ph.D., and Misti Waddell, M.S.,
with Betty Capt, Ph.D., OTR, JoAnn (JJ) Johnson, Ph.D.,
Kristie Pretti-Frontczak, Ph.D., Kristine Slentz, Ph.D.,
and Elizabeth Straka, Ph.D., CCC-SLP

AEPS Curriculum for
Three to Six Years

by Diane Bricker, Ph.D., and Misti Waddell, M.S.,
with Betty Capt, Ph.D., OTR, JoAnn (JJ) Johnson, Ph.D.,
Kristie Pretti-Frontczak, Ph.D., Kristine Slentz, Ph.D.,
and Elizabeth Straka, Ph.D., CCC-SLP

Accompanying web-based management system

AEPSinteractive™ (AEPSi ™) www.aepsi.com

AEPS™
Assessment, Evaluation, and Programming System for Infants and Children
SECOND EDITION

VOLUME 2 — *Test*
Birth to Three Years and Three to Six Years

by

Diane Bricker, Ph.D.
University of Oregon, Eugene

Betty Capt, Ph.D., OTR
University of Oregon, Eugene

and

Kristie Pretti-Frontczak, Ph.D.
Kent State University, Kent, Ohio

with

JoAnn (JJ) Johnson, Ph.D., Kristine Slentz, Ph.D.,
Elizabeth Straka, Ph.D., CCC-SLP, and Misti Waddell, M.S.

·PAUL·H·
BROOKES
PUBLISHING CO.®

Baltimore • London • Sydney

Paul H. Brookes Publishing Co.
Post Office Box 10624
Baltimore, Maryland 21285-0624

www.brookespublishing.com

Typeset by Barton Matheson Willse & Worthington, Baltimore, Maryland.
Manufactured in the United States of America by
Versa Press in East Peoria, Illinois.

The illustration for Objective 3.1 on page 38 is from Bricker, D., & Squires, J. (1999).
*Ages & Stages Questionnaires (ASQ): A parent-completed, child-monitoring
system* (2nd ed.). Baltimore: Paul H. Brookes Publishing Co.; reprinted by permission.

The lyrics on page 93 are from FIVE LITTLE MONKEYS JUMPING ON THE BED by Eileen
Christelow. Copyright © 1989 by Eileen Christelow. Reprinted by permission of Clarion Books/
Houghton Mifflin Company. All right reserved.

The following AEPS forms can be purchased separately in packs:
Child Observation Data Recording Form I: Birth to Three Years, and II: Three to Six Years
Family Report I: Birth to Three Years, and II: Three to Six Years
Child Progress Record I: Birth to Three Years, and II: Three to Six Years

A CD-ROM of printable masters of the AEPS forms is also available, and also includes a Child
Observation Data Recording Form with Criteria for Birth to Three Years and Three to Six Years not
found in any of the volumes. To order, contact Paul H. Brookes Publishing Co.

Please see page ii for a listing of the other volumes in the AEPS series. All AEPS materials are available from Paul H. Brookes Publishing Co., Post Office Box 10624, Baltimore, Maryland 21285-0624
(800-638-3775 or 410-337-9580). Find out more about AEPS on www.brookespublishing.com/aeps.

Fifth printing, December 2007.

Library of Congress Cataloging-in-Publication Data

Assessment, evaluation, and programming system for infants and children
    edited by Diane Bricker . . . (et al.)—2nd ed.
        p.   cm.
    Includes bibliographical references and index.
        ISBN-13: 978-1-55766-563-8 (v. 2) — ISBN 1-55766-562-1 (v. 1) — ISBN 1-55766-563-X (v. 2) —
ISBN 1-55766-564-8 (v. 3) — ISBN 1-55766-565-6 (v. 4)
        1. Assessment, Evaluation, and Programming System.   2. Child development—Testing.
    3. Child development deviations—Diagnosis.
        RJ51.D48 A87 2002
        618.92'0075—dc21
                                                                                2002071124

British Library Cataloguing in Publication data are available from the British Library.

CONTENTS

ABOUT THE AUTHORS

Diane Bricker, Ph.D., Professor, College of Education, and Director, Early Intervention Program, University of Oregon, 5253 University of Oregon, Eugene, Oregon 97403

Diane Bricker is Professor and Associate Dean for Academic Programs, College of Education, at the University of Oregon and a highly respected, well-known authority in the field of early intervention. She has directed a number of national demonstration projects and research efforts focused on examining the efficacy of early intervention; the development of a linked assessment, intervention, and evaluation system; and the study of a comprehensive, parent-focused screening tool. Dr. Bricker directs the Early Intervention Program, Center on Human Development, at the University of Oregon.

Betty Capt, Ph.D., OTR, Research Associate, Early Intervention Program, University of Oregon, 5253 University of Oregon, Eugene, Oregon 97403

Betty Capt is a Research Associate at the Early Intervention Program at the University of Oregon. She also teaches graduate-level coursework in early intervention and provides training nationwide on best practices in assessment and intervention. She is also an occupational therapist and has provided services in early intervention for more than 20 years.

Kristie Pretti-Frontczak, Ph.D., Assistant Professor, Department of Educational Foundations and Special Services, Kent State University, 405 White Hall, Kent, Ohio 44242

Kristie Pretti-Frontczak is Assistant Professor in the Department of Educational Foundations and Special Services at Kent State University. She received her doctorate in early intervention from the University of Oregon and has extensive experience in preparing preservice and in-service personnel to use an activity-based approach to working with young children and their families. Dr. Pretti-Frontczak also directs the Early Childhood Intervention Specialist Program at Kent State University where she is responsible for preparing preservice teachers to work with children from birth to age 8. She frequently provides training and technical assistance to programs across the United States of America interested in the *Assessment, Evaluation, and Programming System for Infants and Children* (AEPS) and activity-based intervention (ABI). Her line of research also centers on the treatment validity of the AEPS and efficacy of ABI.

JoAnn (JJ) Johnson, Ph.D., Director, Research and Educational Planning Center and Nevada University Center for Excellence in Developmental Disabilities, University of Nevada–Reno, Reno, Nevada 89557

Kristine Slentz, Ph.D., Professor and Chair, Special Education Department, Western Washington University, Miller Hall 318b, Mail Stop 9090, Bellingham, Washington 98226

Elizabeth Straka, Ph.D., CCC-SLP, Consultant, New England Early Intervention Consulting, 58 Turtle Cove Lane, Wells, Maine 04090

Misti Waddell, M.S., Senior Research Assistant/Project Coordinator, Early Intervention Program, University of Oregon, 5253 University of Oregon, Eugene, Oregon 97403

ACKNOWLEDGMENTS

The *Assessment, Evaluation, and Programming System for Infants and Children* (AEPS) is the culmination of years of work by an array of thinkers, developers, users, and evaluators. One strength of this curriculum-based measure has been the multiple theories, perspectives, frameworks, and needs that have shaped its continuing evolution since its inception in 1974. Trying to organize this multiplicity of perspectives into a conceptually cohesive approach and manageable test and curriculum has been a significant challenge that has admittedly resulted in uneven success. From the beginning, the actualization of the ideals that underlie the AEPS (i.e., the development of a reliable and valid measure that yields results directly applicable to the development of functional and appropriate goals and intervention content and that can monitor child progress) has outstripped our collective abilities to reach these ideals. However, a comparison between where we began in 1974 and where we are today with this second edition of the AEPS offers solid proof of important progress toward reaching those ideals. The thousands of hours that have been spent in the refinements of the AEPS Test and associated curricular materials have produced important modifications, expansions, and changes in the second edition of the AEPS. The "perfect" test and teaching materials still beckon far beyond our collective reach; however, we believe that the second edition of the AEPS moves us closer to actualizing those original ideals. We believe that using the second edition of the AEPS will yield accurate, valid, and reliable test outcomes; will produce appropriate, timely, functional, generalizable and measurable goals; will support effective intervention efforts; and will enable the efficient monitoring of child progress.

The various changes incorporated into the second edition of the AEPS are the result of a collective effort of the seven authors who brought their own experience and knowledge to the discussions, as well as feedback they received from hundreds of other professionals and caregivers who have used the first edition of the AEPS. Users' suggestions and noted deficiencies served as powerful instigators of the changes made in the second edition, and we are grateful to the many individuals who have provided their perspectives, feedback, and thoughtful ideas about improving the AEPS. We are particularly indebted to our colleagues Jane Squires, David Allen, Jantina Clifford, Alise Carter, Naomi Rahn, and Natalya McComas for providing insightful observations, helping with material development, and generally keeping us centered on the task.

The size, complexity, and interrelated nature of the AEPS Test and curricular materials have required iterative reviews, readings, and editing. Dave Allen, James Jacobson, Kate Ray, Renata Smith, and Erika Hinds helped with these tasks. This multilevel and nested project has been like assembling a jigsaw puzzle. Karen Lawrence has been extraordinary in checking the content of each piece and getting the pieces assembled and sequenced in the right order. Her attention to detail has been enormously helpful. We are grateful to her for her ongoing assistance in completing this truly challenging work. In addition, the staff of Paul H. Brookes Publishing Co. has been of great assistance by their commitment to this large and complex project, their openness to change, their responsiveness to requests, and their positive and supportive feedback. The AEPS began as a collective effort, continues as a collective effort, and likely will continue to evolve as a collective effort.

AEPS™

**Assessment, Evaluation,
and Programming System
for Infants and Children**

SECOND EDITION

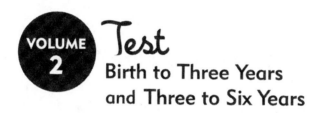

VOLUME 2

Test

**Birth to Three Years
and Three to Six Years**

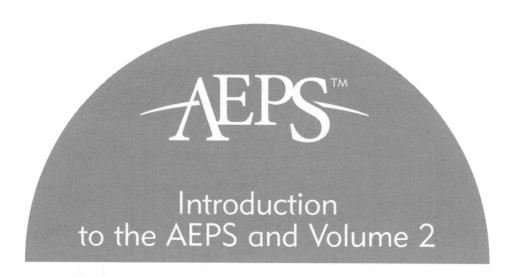

Introduction to the AEPS and Volume 2

The importance of early experience for young children has long been recognized and has been the foundation for early intervention programs designed for young children who have or who are at risk for disabilities. Early intervention programs have evolved into comprehensive approaches that produce positive change in the lives of participating children and their families. In large measure, the increasingly positive outcomes engendered by early intervention programs have occurred because of the growing sophistication of personnel, curricular materials, and assessment/evaluation tools. Previous approaches that treat program components as isolated and unrelated units are being replaced by approaches that systematically link the major components of assessment, goal development, intervention, and evaluation. The *Assessment, Evaluation, and Programming System for Infants and Children (AEPS)*™ is one such linked approach.

This is the second volume of the AEPS series. Figure 1 shows the four volumes of the series and briefly lists the content of each volume. The primary content of Volume 2 is the AEPS Test items and their associated criteria for Birth to Three Years and Three to Six Years.

WHAT IS THE AEPS?

The AEPS offers a variety of related materials that enhance the link between assessment information, targeted goals, intervention activities, and evaluation strategies. The AEPS is referred to as a system because its components work together to assist interventionists and caregivers in developing functional and coordinated assessment, goal development, intervention, and evaluation activities for young children who have or who are at risk for disabilities. The AEPS is a comprehensive and linked system that includes assessment/evaluation, curricular, and family participation components for the developmental range from birth to 6 years. The AEPS is divided into two developmental levels—Birth to Three Years and Three to Six Years.

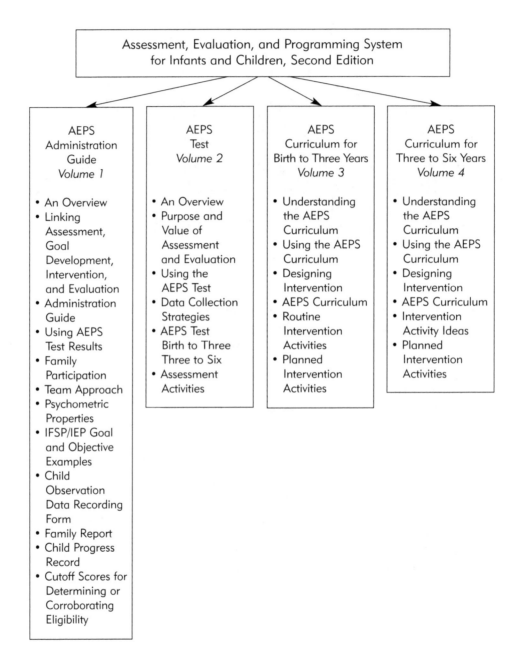

Figure 2. Four volumes of the *Assessment, Evaluation, and Programming System for Infants and Children, Second Edition.*

Volume 1 presents information on the conceptual and organizational structure of the AEPS, how to get started using the system, components of a linked system, interpretation and use of test outcomes, family involvement strategies in the assessment/evaluation process, and team collaboration suggestions for using the system. Also in Volume 1, a new strategy for using AEPS test results to corroborate standardized, norm-referenced test findings for eligibility determination is described.

Volume 2 contains the AEPS Test items for Birth to Three Years and Three to Six Years divided into six developmental areas: Fine Motor, Gross Motor, Adaptive, Cognitive, Social-Communication, and Social. The content is developmentally sequenced beginning with simple skills and moving to more advanced skills. The AEPS Test items only include functional skills that are potentially appropriate intervention targets. Volume 2 also contains Assessment Activities that are simple scripts to guide the assessment of a range of AEPS Test items during specific activities.

Volumes 3 and 4 contain the curricular materials for the developmental ranges of Birth to Three Years and Three to Six Years respectively. In addition, these volumes contain a variety of intervention activities appropriate for a range of children.

The AEPS is appropriate for children who present a broad range of intervention needs, including infants and young children with identified developmental disabilities such as Down syndrome, spina bifida, and cerebral palsy. In addition, the AEPS can be used with children who have chronic health conditions, who have general developmental delays, and for those who live in high-risk conditions (e.g., poverty, parents who are substance users).

Children with severe disabilities will likely have a team (e.g., occupational therapist, physical therapist, communication specialist, special educator, service coordinator) who will be involved in developing strategies for intervention. The AEPS lends itself well to a team approach because it permits input from a variety of specialists and provides a structure for the coordination of information gleaned from those different sources.

The following chapter provides more detail on the content and organization of Volume 2 and describes the changes made in the second edition of the AEPS.

SECTION

1

Using Volume 2

1

The AEPS: An Overview

Volume 2 of the AEPS contains the assessment/evaluation test items for the birth to three and three to six year levels. In addition, Volume 2 contains information on the purpose and value of assessment and evaluation and how to use the AEPS Test. This chapter provides a brief overview of the second edition of the AEPS series and discusses the importance of reading and understanding the information in Volume 1 (which recounts the historical development of this curriculum-based measure and a description of the first edition of the series) prior to using the test items contained in Volume 2. The need for using Volumes 1 and 2 in tandem cannot be overemphasized.

THE SECOND EDITION OF THE AEPS

Since the publication of the first edition of the *AEPS Measurement* and *Curriculum for Birth to Three Years* in 1993 and the *AEPS Measurement* and *Curriculum for Three to Six Years* in 1996, data and information on the usefulness of the AEPS system to professionals and caregivers have been collected. Studying this information has led to a number of changes in the second edition of the AEPS. These changes are of three types: organizational, content, and format. Each of these changes is briefly described in this chapter. It is important to note that the basic purpose and content of the AEPS remain the same; that is, the AEPS remains a curriculum-based measurement system that links assessment, goal development, intervention, and evaluation activities.

A review of Figure 1 (contained in the introduction to this volume) highlights the organizational structure of the second edition. To reduce redundancy, the foundational information for understanding and using the AEPS has been combined into one volume. Volume 1 presents information on the conceptual and organizational structure of the AEPS, how to get started using the system, components of a linked system, interpretation of test outcomes, family involvement in the assessment/evaluation process, and team collaboration strategies for using the system.

Volume 2 contains the test items for the birth to three year level and the three to six year level in six developmental areas: Fine Motor, Gross Motor, Adaptive, Cognitive, Social-Communication, and Social. The majority of AEPS Test items (i.e., goals/objectives) have remained unchanged from the first edition. Minor changes (e.g., word changes) were undertaken to improve the clarity of a few items and their criteria; only a small number of items were extensively rewritten. As shown in Table 1, items were eliminated and added. The most significant changes in the birth to three year level occurred in the Cognitive Area in which nine items were added. In the three to six year level the greatest changes occurred in the Social Area in which 14 items were added and in the Cognitive Area in which 38 items were eliminated. In the latter case, content was not deleted, rather, several items were combined; for example, in the first edition, demonstrating understanding of color, size, and shape was presented as three separate goals, whereas in the second edition, these three goals were combined into one goal with associated objectives that separately address understanding of color, size, and shape. As shown in Table 1, the total number of items for the birth to three year level increased from 228 to 249, whereas the total number of items for the three to six year level decreased from 245 to 217.

Volumes 3 and 4 of the second edition contain the curricular material for the developmental range birth to three years and three to six years respectively. An important change in these volumes has been expanded descriptions of how to use the AEPS curricular materials with an activity-based approach to intervention. As with the AEPS Test, however, the basic content of the AEPS curricula has remained the same.

A final change across volumes is format. In both age ranges of the AEPS Test, redundant directions were removed from specific items and placed into a general section titled "Caution." In the curriculum for birth to three years, intervention strategies have been consolidated, which has reduced the redundancy of the volume. Finally, tabs to delineate each area have been included to enhance the ease of locating test items and curricular content.

The changes introduced in the second edition of the AEPS are designed to improve its usefulness to interventionists and caregivers and to clarify procedures for its use. The underlying philosophy of the AEPS and its basic intent remain unchanged.

THE SECOND EDITION

A major purpose behind the re-organization of the material in the second edition of the AEPS is to assist caregivers and professional staff in its use. By re-formatting the item directions, the size of the AEPS Tests for Birth to Three and Three to Six Years has been reduced, permitting their combination into one volume. The combination should assist the AEPS user in administering the test in a more efficient and effective manner.

Combining test items for birth to three and three to six years into one volume required that information on how to use the AEPS Test and the test administration guidelines be placed in a separate volume. It is the intent of the AEPS developers that Volumes 1 and 2 be used together. Administering the

Table 1. AEPS item changes from the first to second edition

Area	Birth to Three			Three to Six		
	Number of items in first edition	Number of items in second edition	Change	Number of items in first edition	Number of items in second edition	Change
Fine Motor	28	33	+5	14	15	+1
Gross Motor	55	55	0	18	17	−1
Adaptive	32	32	0	39	35	−4
Cognitive	49	58	+9	92	54	−38
Social-Communication	42	46	+4	49	49	0
Social	22	25	+3	33	47	+14
Total	228	249	+21	245	217	−28

items in Volume 2 without reading and understanding the wealth of information in Volume 1 will likely lead to misuse of the measurement system and invalid child outcomes.

Prior to using the AEPS Test items contained in Volume 2, the AEPS user should carefully read Chapters 1–6 in Volume 1. Chapter 1 in Volume 1 provides an overview of the AEPS, who should use it, and why. This chapter also contains guidelines on how first-time users of the AEPS can begin to use the system in an efficient manner. Chapter 2 presents a discussion of the importance of linking assessment, goal development, intervention, and evaluation activities. This linked approach provides the conceptual framework for the AEPS and is important for users to understand. Chapter 3 provides detailed information on the content and organization of the AEPS and guidelines for administration and scoring procedures. Using AEPS test results to develop goals/objectives and IFSP/IEP intervention plans is presented in Chapter 4. Chapter 5 describes the procedures and AEPS materials specifically designed to involve parents and other caregivers in assessment, goal development, intervention, and evaluation activities. The final chapter offers a team collaboration approach for using the AEPS. In addition, a number of vignettes are presented throughout Volume 1 that provide examples of how to use the AEPS with children and families.

Volume 2 is divided into three sections. In the first section, Chapters 1, 2, and 3 highlight information critical to the AEPS user. The material contained in these chapters should not be seen as a replacement of the information contained in Volume 1. Chapter 4 describes individual and group assessment strategies. The second section of Volume 2 contains the AEPS Test items for Birth to Three Years. Section III of Volume 2 contains the AEPS Test items for Three to Six Years. Each level contains test items for the six developmental areas targeted by the AEPS. Appendix A contains sample Assessment Activities.

2

The Purpose and Value of Assessment and Evaluation

Although many people use the terms *assessment* and *evaluation* interchangeably, we believe that it is important to draw a distinction between them because these terms represent two different and important concepts and processes. In early intervention/early childhood special education (EI/ECSE), *assessment* refers to the concept and process of determining a baseline or current status in targeted areas. Most often, the assessment process is focused on determining children's or caregiver's skill and knowledge. *Evaluation,* however, refers to the concept and process of comparing a child's performance in order to determine eligibility or progress. In the AEPS, the evaluation process is focused on comparing children's performance or knowledge acquisition before intervention begins and then at later predetermined times following treatment or intervention activities.

PURPOSE OF ASSESSMENT AND EVALUATION

Assessment activities are designed to determine and describe current performance and knowledge, whereas evaluation activities are designed to make comparisons over time. Given these definitions, the purpose of curriculum-based assessment is to determine children's current developmental repertoires across a range of important areas of behavior. Specifically, such assessment is used to determine the skills and information children have and under what conditions they are used. In addition, assessment procedures should determine the next level of skills and information that children should be acquiring; this information is crucial in determining intervention targets. The information necessary to develop an appropriate IFSP/IEP document should be generated by the assessment activities.

The purpose of evaluation is to compare children's behavioral repertoires at different points over time following intervention or to monitor progress toward family outcomes; for example, following 3 months of intervention, the interventionist's measurement of change in child performance on selected

goals and comparison of the performance to a previous measure would constitute an evaluation of child progress. Recommended practice requires that children's repertoires in target areas be measured and compared at least quarterly
to ensure adequate progress toward goals.

THE VALUE OF ASSESSMENT AND EVALUATION

Discussing the value of assessment and evaluation is important because many
EI/ECSE personnel do not systematically use objective measures to assess children's entry behaviors, nor do they use sound measurement strategies to evaluate performance over time. Programs that do not conduct objective assessment
and evaluation activities offer many reasons for this, including a lack of time,
limited financial resources, inappropriate measurement tools, and inadequately
trained personnel. We believe that while these challenges do exist, program personnel need to engage in systematic assessment and evaluation activities.

An example may help explain our reasoning. Suppose you have just
discovered that you have a winning lottery ticket; however, to receive your
million-dollar prize you must present the winning ticket to an office located
in Denver, Colorado, within 2 weeks. You then realize that you are standing
in a wooded area without any signs to indicate your location. You do not know
the state or county in which you stand. Because you do not know your present location, your two choices are to remain where you are, hoping to be discovered, or to begin walking in some direction. Let us say that you begin walking north. If you are located in Arizona, then you might run into Denver;
however, if you are located in Minnesota, then you will miss Denver completely. If you begin walking east, then you might hit Denver if you are located
in Oregon, but if you are in Missouri, then you will again miss your target
completely. Even once you are headed in the right general direction, you may
make many detours because you lack precise information on where you are
and a reasonable set of directions to lead you to Denver. You may eventually
get to Denver, but long after the lottery office is closed and your winnings are
being spent by someone who knew where he or she was and had a system to
measure his or her progress toward Denver.

Failing to establish children's baseline skills, select goals, and map how
to reach those goals places children and families in wooded areas with little
chance of successful escape. How can early interventionists select appropriate
goals/objectives for children and families if they do not know what children
can and cannot do and what families see as problems that need remedies? Fur-
thermore, how can interventionists determine whether children and families
are making systematic progress toward selected goals/objectives if their progress is not evaluated over time?

Without comprehensive information regarding children's behavioral repertoires and interests, personnel simply cannot select and implement appropriate interventions. Beginning intervention without adequate assessment information is likely to lead to moving in the wrong direction and making many
unnecessary detours. This, of course, results in wasted resources and time for
children, families, and interventionists.

Equally important is the systematic evaluation of child progress over time. Without monitoring progress toward goals/objectives, intervention personnel and caregivers have no way of determining whether intervention is effective and change is in order. Again, to not evaluate change over time will likely result in wasted efforts and the poor use of limited resources.

SUMMARY

Assessment and evaluation of children and families in EI/ECSE programs is essential, and curriculum-based measures such as the AEPS can be of great assistance in both providing a broad range of relevant information on a child's entry repertoire and then in monitoring child progress toward established goals/objectives. Using the AEPS should enhance efforts of the interventionist, teacher, and specialist to ensure the effective use of resources and maximum progress for children and their families.

3

Using the AEPS Test

A linked assessment, goal development, intervention, and evaluation approach is predicated on having a measurement instrument that permits the collection of program-related performance data on children that can be used across these four activities.

An assessment/evaluation measure should meet certain criteria in order to be appropriate for infants and young children who are at risk for or who have disabilities and to provide useful intervention and evaluation information. Instruments designed to assess children, monitor child progress, and assist in program evaluation should

- Be used by those people who interact with the child on a regular basis (e.g., interventionists, assistants, parents) in familiar settings (e.g., home, classroom, child care)

- Reflect the curricular content of intervention efforts

- Provide a logical developmental sequence of items that can be used as intervention guidelines

- Accommodate a range of disabilities

- Specify performance criteria that indicate if a child has a particular skill and if the skill is a functional part of the child's repertoire

- Have reliability and validity data to support its use

The AEPS Test is a curriculum-based measure developed for use by direct services personnel (e.g., center-based interventionists, child care workers, home visitors) and specialists (e.g., communication specialists, occupational therapists, physical therapists, psychologists) to assess and evaluate the skills and abilities of infants and young children who are at risk for or who have disabilities. The AEPS Test was designed to yield appropriate information for the development of IFSP/IEP goals, intervention content, and evaluation procedures.

15

Items on the AEPS Test cover two developmental levels: birth to three years and three to six years. Items are focused on determining a child's skill level across early critical processes. The AEPS Test is generally appropriate for children whose chronological age is from 3 months to 9 years. Significant modification may be necessary, however, in the wording of the items, criteria, and suggested testing procedures to make them appropriate for a child who is chronologically older than 6 years of age.

TARGET POPULATION

The AEPS Test was designed to be used with children who are at risk for or who have disabilities. The AEPS Test has been successfully used with children who have Down syndrome, cerebral palsy, central nervous system disorders, seizure disorders, sensory impairments, and general developmental delays, as well as children who are typically developing but at risk (e.g., those with adolescent parents, those with substance-using parents, those with medical problems).

Interventionists and specialists have also used the AEPS Test with children who have severe impairments. Successful use of the test with this population may require some general modifications. For children whose chronological age exceeds 6 years, items should be carefully evaluated to ensure their appropriateness for elementary-age children.

CONTENT AND ORGANIZATION OF THE AEPS TEST

Conducting assessment and evaluation with the AEPS Test allows interventionists to generate a comprehensive profile of the child's behavior in familiar environments, as opposed to a narrow description of one aspect of the child's behavior. To collect comprehensive information on the child's developmental status, six broad curricular areas are included: Fine Motor, Gross Motor, Adaptive, Cognitive, Social-Communication, and Social. Each area encompasses a particular set of skills, behaviors, or information that is traditionally seen as related developmental phenomena called *strands*; for example, behaviors relating to movement in standing and walking are grouped in the Balance and Mobility strand in the Gross Motor Area of the AEPS Test for Birth to Three Years. An overview of each level's six areas and their associated strands is provided in Table 2.

Items on the AEPS Test are arranged to facilitate the assessment of a child's ability to perform a particular behavior within a developmental sequence of skills. Each strand contains a series of test items referred to as *goals and objectives*. These items can be used to write IFSPs/IEPs. The objectives represent components of the goals or more discrete skills and enable the user to accurately pinpoint a child's level within a specific skill sequence.

The number of strands varies by area, as shown in Table 2. Strands and goals are arranged from easier or developmentally earlier skills to more diffi-

Table 2. Overview of the areas and strands for the two levels of the AEPS Test

Areas		Birth to Three strands		Three to Six strands
Fine Motor	A. B.	Reach, Grasp, and Release Functional Use of Fine Motor Skills	A. B.	Bilateral Motor Coordination Emergent Writing
Gross Motor	A. B. C. D.	Movement and Locomotion in Supine and Prone Position Balance in Sitting Balance and Mobility Play Skills	A. B.	Balance and Mobility Play Skills
Adaptive	A. B. C.	Feeding Personal Hygiene Undressing	A. B. C.	Mealtime Personal Hygiene Dressing and Undressing
Cognitive	A. B. C. D. E. F. G.	Sensory Stimuli Object Permanence Causality Imitation Problem Solving Interaction with Objects Early Concepts	A. B. C. D. E. F. G. H.	Concepts Categorizing Sequencing Recalling Events Problem Solving Play Premath Phonological Awareness and Emergent Reading
Social- Communication	A. B. C. D.	Prelinguistic Communicative Interactions Transition to Words Comprehension of Words and Sentences Production of Social- Communicative Signals, Words, and Sentences	A. B.	Social-Communicative Interactions Production of Words, Phrases, and Sentences
Social	A. B. C.	Interaction with Familiar Adults Interaction with Environment Interaction with Peers	A. B. C. D.	Interaction with Others Participation Interaction with Environment Knowledge of Self and Others

cult or developmentally more advanced skills whenever possible. The objectives listed under each goal are arranged in a reverse sequence—the most difficult items occur first and the less difficult items follow sequentially. This was done to facilitate test administration. If a child performs a more advanced objective within a sequence of objectives (e.g., jumps in place within the developmental sequence of play skills), then the assessment of earlier objectives within the sequence (e.g., jumps from platform; balances on one foot) is generally unnecessary. This procedure makes assessment more efficient and generally holds true unless the child's behavioral repertoire appears to be uneven (i.e., the child is inconsistent and performs a variety of splinter skills). In this case, assessment of a broader range of items is in order. For some strands, objectives associated with a particular goal may occur concurrently rather than hierarchically. In these cases, all objectives should be assessed; for example, if a child is able to prepare food for eating, then assessment of the ability to spread with knife, pour liquids, and serve food with utensils may also need to be assessed. The hierarchical arrangement of easy to more difficult strands, goals, and objectives is shown in Figure 2.

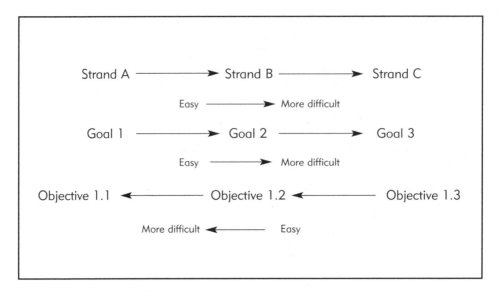

Figure 2. Hierarchical arrangement of strands, goals, and objectives on the AEPS Test.

The identification system associated with the strands (e.g., A, B, C), goals (e.g., 1, 2, 3), and objectives (e.g., 1.1, 1.2, 1.3) reflects this sequential arrangement and has been included to assist the test user in locating and referring to items. The organizational structure of the strands, goals, and objectives is presented in Figure 3. More detailed information on the AEPS Test and its administration is contained in Volume 1, Chapter 3.

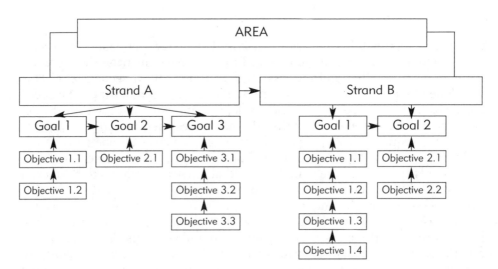

Figure 3. Organizational structure of items on the AEPS Test.

COLLABORATIVE TEAM ASSESSMENT

Programs that provide services and care to young children have a variety of staffing patterns. Many programs have more than one interdisciplinary team specialist who is regularly available to children and families. Participation by these specialists in the administration of curriculum-based assessments, such as the AEPS Test, is encouraged. Inclusion of specialists helps ensure the efficient and comprehensive completion of the programmatic assessment for children. The team members may choose to participate in group, center-based assessment by observing and interacting with the children at particular times; for example, the communication specialist might record a language sample on the Social-Communication Observation Form during snack time, whereas the physical or occupational therapist might complete the Fine Motor and Gross Motor portions on the Child Observation Data Recording Form during free play. Another alternative is for the specialists to observe and score the areas pertinent to their areas of expertise while a child care worker moves children through a series of assessment activities.

To increase the awareness of the strengths and needs of children across developmental areas, results should be compiled and shared among the team members. Such sharing also helps eliminate the redundancy and inconsistency that occur when professionals complete separate assessments. Incorporating the observations of the specialists and interventionists into one assessment protocol leads to more efficient and functional intervention planning. Chapter 6 in Volume 1 discusses team collaboration approaches in using the AEPS in greater detail.

SUMMARY

The information contained in this chapter assists in understanding the general features of the AEPS Test that distinguish it from other available instruments. The overall organization and content of the AEPS Test are described to assist in appreciating its structure and coverage. Specific administration guidelines are contained in Volume 1.

4

Data Collection Strategies

The comprehensive and detailed coverage provided by the AEPS Test requires thought and planning. Knowing and understanding the AEPS Test items and their associated criteria is critical to accurate administration and scoring. Consequently, prior to using the AEPS Test, it is essential that the user be familiar with the material contained in Volume 1—the administration guide. In addition, this chapter describes a set of data collection strategies that may be particularly useful for the new user of the AEPS Test. The chapter is divided into the following three sections:

1. Using Descriptive Records
2. Using the Child Observation Data Recording Form
3. Data Collection: Variations in Number of Children and Areas

USING DESCRIPTIVE RECORDS

Until becoming familiar with the AEPS Test items and the Child Observation Data Recording Form, users may find that writing a descriptive record of children's behaviors across activities is preferable. While observing children who are engaged in routine or planned activities in center-based settings or at home, a variety of methods can be used to record observations. The interventionist or caregiver could use a note pad or sticky notes to jot observations; a notebook or clipboard could be placed in each play setting or room for the quick entry of descriptive notes.

It is important to transfer the descriptive information collected to the Child Observation Data Recording Form on a regular basis (e.g., at the end of each day). The timely transfer of information will help ensure an accurate completion of AEPS Test items. Accurate scoring of the items is also dependent on careful reading and use of each scored item's criteria. To ensure maximum accuracy and efficiency, users of the AEPS Test will want to begin scoring the Child Observation Data Recording Form directly as soon as possible.

USING THE CHILD OBSERVATION DATA RECORDING FORM

The most accurate and efficient method for scoring the AEPS Test is to use the specially designed Child Observation Data Recording Form (see Volume 1, Appendix C). This form is ideal for those wanting to document a single child's development over time. Users should note, however, that it is necessary for them to refer to the criteria found in Sections II and III of Volume 2 to determine the score associated with a child's present level of performance. These forms can be purchased in a packet or on a CD-Rom from Paul H. Brookes Publishing Co. The CD-Rom includes a bonus Child Observation Data Recording Form with Criteria for Birth to Three Years and Three to Six Years.

DATA COLLECTION:
VARIATIONS IN NUMBER OF CHILDREN AND AREAS

Whether using descriptive records or a Child Observation Data Recording Form, assessment information can be collected in at least four different ways: one child–one area (e.g., Cognitive); one child–multiple areas (e.g., Cognitive and Social); several children–one area; and several children–multiple areas. New users of the AEPS Test are advised to begin with assessing one child–one area and, once comfortable, to move to assessing one child across areas. After becoming familiar with the AEPS Test, the user can shift to the more efficient methods of assessing multiple children in one area and finally to assessing multiple children across areas.

One Child–One Area

When assessing one child in one area, center-based and home activities can be structured so that materials and equipment are available that focus on that particular area; for example, assessing the Gross Motor Area might involve having riding toys, steps, and room to run and jump. For assessing the Cognitive Area, an activity might be planned that provides the child many opportunities to demonstrate his or her understanding of concepts such as color, shape, and size. As the child engages in the activity or activities, the interventionist or specialist can take descriptive notes or, preferably, score the Child Observation Data Recording Form in the target area.

One Child–Multiple Areas

The more efficient method for assessing one child is across areas simultaneously, but this requires familiarity with a range of AEPS Test items; for example, while assessing a child's gross motor skills, the interventionist may also be able to assess his or her language and social skills (e.g., the level of expressive language used during play and the type of interaction with peers observed).

Several Children–One Area

There are obvious advantages to assessing more than one child at a time; however, assessing several children at the same time requires practice and familiarity with the AEPS Test items. For example, if three children are in a gross motor play area, then the interventionist could observe and record all three children's gross motor skills as they engage in a variety of activities. It may be that in assessing several children simultaneously, not all test items will be addressed for all children. This outcome requires that the interventionist follow up with planned activities to elicit missed items. The AEPS Assessment Activities contained in Appendix A of this volume are useful for this purpose.

Several Children–Multiple Areas

The most efficient assessment strategy is to assess several children across a range of developmental areas; however, using this strategy requires considerable practice and knowledge of the AEPS Test. Interventionists who chose this data collection strategy will want to consider using the AEPS Assessment Activities contained in Appendix A of this volume.

SUMMARY

The purpose of this chapter is to suggest a set of data collection strategies that can be employed by AEPS Test users. In particular, we recommend that new users of the test consider beginning with simple assessment strategies that focus on one child and one area. As test users become more experienced, we recommend that they then begin using strategies that, although more complex, are clearly more efficient.

SECTION

II

AEPS Test: Birth to Three Years

OVERVIEW OF THE AEPS TEST: BIRTH TO THREE YEARS

The AEPS Test: Birth to Three Years covers the developmental range from 1 month to 3 years and is generally appropriate for children whose chronological age is from 3 months to 6 years. The AEPS Test is composed of six areas; each area encompasses a particular set of skills, behaviors, or information that is traditionally seen as developmentally related.

- **Fine Motor Area:** Items in this area assess arm and hand movements that encompass reaching and grasping and object manipulation skills.

- **Gross Motor Area:** Items in this area assess the ability to maintain stability in various positions (balance), to move from one position into another, and to use coordinated play skills.

- **Adaptive Area:** Items in this area assess eating, drinking, self-care, and undressing skills.

- **Cognitive Area:** Items in this area assess reactions to sensory input, object permanence, causality, imitation, problem solving, and the understanding of early concepts.

- **Social-Communication Area:** Items in this area assess receptive, expressive, and social use of communication skills.

- **Social Area:** Items in this area assess interactions with adults, siblings, and peers, as well as meeting physical needs.

TEST ORGANIZATION AND SCORING

Before using the AEPS Test, the user should carefully read and review the material contained in Chapter 3 of Volume 1. Chapter 3 provides detailed information on the content and organization of the AEPS Test. In addition, scoring criteria, notes, and options are discussed in Chapter 3. Consequently, these topics are reviewed only briefly in the current section.

Organizational Structure

The AEPS Test: Birth to Three Years addresses six developmental areas: Fine Motor, Gross Motor, Adaptive, Cognitive, Social-Communication, and Social.

Each area is divided into strands, which in turn contain a series of goals with associated objectives. Each strand and goal/objective has an index letter or number for easy referral. Strands are identified with capital letters (e.g., Strand A, Strand B, Strand C). Goals are identified with whole numbers (e.g., 1, 2, 3) and are listed under their respective strands. Objectives are listed under their respective goals and are identified with a decimal number (e.g., 1.1, 1.2, 1.3) that reflects the goal number. For example, objectives associated with Goal 3 are indexed as 3.1, 3.2, and 3.3.

Item Criterion and Scoring

Each AEPS Test item is accompanied by a performance criterion. The test user should use the criterion as the standard for scoring the child's response. A three-point scoring option (i.e., 2, 1, 0) should be employed consistently across items. To determine whether the child's response should be scored 2, 1, or 0, specific criteria are provided for each AEPS Test item (i.e., for each goal/objective). It is essential to compare children's performance with each item's criterion before recording a score. Criteria are found under the description of each test item. Table 3 presents a summary of scoring guidelines when information is collected through direct test procedures and observation.

It should be emphasized that arranging antecedent conditions to help elicit responses from children does not necessarily constitute direct testing; for example, placing silverware within a child's reach to assess eating skills is not direct testing. Having available and accessible objects of different colors, sizes, and configurations to assess a child's early concept understanding would not be considered direct testing. Rather, *direct testing* refers to conducting specific trial-by-trial procedures generally apart from routine or play activities in which specific and direct antecedents are given; for example, the child is repeatedly shown a set of pictures and asked to name them.

In addition to the three-option scoring codes, notes are provided to allow users to record other important information about a child's performance on AEPS Test items; for example, a child may use adaptive equipment such as a communication board to perform an item of labeling objects and events. Because the child can demonstrate the concept of labeling independently and consistently, the item is scored 2, but it is also scored with a note (i.e., M = modification/adaptation in this case). Notes alert teams to important information that should be considered when interpreting AEPS Test information, designing subsequent intervention plans, and conducting future evaluations. Modifications of items for children with disabilities is encouraged; however, when such modifications occur, they should be noted. A description of the six notes and associated scoring guidelines is contained in Table 4.

Table 3.   Scoring guidelines for observation and direct test procedures

Score	Description of performance
Observation	
2 = Consistently meets criterion	Child consistently performs the item as specified in the criterion.
	Child performs the item independently.
	Behavior is a functional part of the child's repertoire.
	Child uses the skill across time, materials, settings, and people.
1 = Inconsistently meets criterion	Child does not consistently perform the item as specified in the criterion.
	Child performs the item with assistance.
	Child does not perform all components of the item or does not meet all aspects of the specified criterion (i.e., the behavior is emerging).
	Child performs the item only under specific situations or conditions (i.e., with certain people or in certain settings).
0 = Does not meet criterion	Child does not yet perform the item as specified in the criterion when given repeated opportunities or assistance or when modifications and adaptations are made.
	Child was not observed performing the item because it is not expected based on knowledge of development (e.g., the child's chronological age is 6 months and he or she would not be expected to perform such items as categorizing similar objects, copying simple shapes, or walking up and down stairs).
Direct test	
2 = Consistently meets criterion	Child performs the item as specified in the criterion on at least two out of three trials.
	Child performs the item independently on two out of three trials.
	Child uses the skill on two out of three trials across time, materials, settings, and people.
1 = Inconsistently meets criterion	Child performs the item as specified in the criterion on one out of three trials.
	Child performs the item with assistance on one out of three trials.
	Child performs only portions of the item or certain aspects of the specified criterion on one out of three trials.
	Child performs the item under one situation or one set of conditions.
0 = Does not meet criterion	Child does not yet perform the item as specified in the criterion on zero out of three trials when assistance is provided or when modifications and adaptations are made.
	Child was not observed performing the item because it is not expected based on knowledge of development (e.g., the child's chronological age is 6 months and he or she would not be expected to perform such items as categorizing similar objects, copying simple shapes, or walking up and down stairs), thus no trials are given.

Table 4. Notes, definitions, and scoring guidelines

Note	Definitions and scoring guidelines
A	**Assistance provided**

When a child is provided with some form of *assistance*, an A should be noted in the space next to the performance score box. If assistance is provided, then the only scores allowed are 1 and 0 because a score of 2 indicates full independent performance. Assistance includes any direct verbal or physical prompt, cue, or model that assists the child in initiating or performing the desired behavior. A general direction given to the child to initiate the behavior is not considered assistance. For example, the directive, "Put on your coat" is not considered assistance, but physically holding out the coat and helping the child insert his or her arms is assistance for the AEPS Test item Puts on Front-Opening Garment.

| B | **Behavior interfered** |

At times, a child's behavior may interfere with the demonstration of the desired skill. In such cases, the item may be scored 1 or 0 with a B noted next to the performance score. This note indicates that the child may have the skill, but disruptive or noncompliant behavior interfered with its demonstration.

| D | **Direct test** |

When the examiner directly elicits a behavior, a D is noted next to the performance score and the guidelines for determining the score presented in Table 3 should be followed.

| M | **Modification/adaptation** |

At times, an examiner may need to modify the stated *criteria* (e.g., rate or mode of response) or adapt the *environment/materials* (e.g., adaptive equipment is necessary) to assess children with sensory or motor disabilities. When *modifications* are made in gathering child performance information, an M is noted next to the performance score and a 2, 1, or 0 is used.

| Q | **Quality of performance** |

At times, a child is able to perform a skill independently, but the team feels the quality of the performance hinders the ability to meet criteria. At other times, a child is able to meet or partially meet the stated criteria, but the team wishes to continue strengthening the quality of performance. When the quality of the performance is in question, teams are encouraged to use a Q in the notes accompanied by a score of 2 or 1.

| R | **Report** |

When an item is assessed by *report*, an R is noted next to the performance score. Report is used under one of three conditions:

- When assessment information is collected by another person or documented source (e.g., written evaluation), the item is scored 2, 1, or 0, and an R is noted.
- When the item is judged inappropriate because it assesses a primitive or developmentally easier response (e.g., sucking on a nipple when the child is able to drink from a cup), the item is scored 2 and an R is noted.
- When the item is judged inappropriate because it is too advanced or beyond the child's developmental level (e.g., walking when the child is unable to stand), the item is scored 0 and an R is noted.

TEST MATERIALS

No standard or required set of materials or objects is necessary for the administration of the AEPS Test items. Commonly available toys and objects can be used in the administration of all items. Toys and other objects that are of interest to the child are likely to produce more accurate assessment information than using materials that are of limited interest to the child. Therefore, before administering test items, it is essential to talk with caregivers to determine what types of materials the child prefers. It is also important to select age-appropriate materials. Suggested materials for each developmental area are listed below.

Materials for AEPS Test: Birth to Three Years

Fine Motor

To assess reaching and grasping
  Mobile, crib gym, rattle, squeeze-toy
  Block, wooden bead, small ball
  Pea-size objects (e.g., raisins, Cheerios, buttons)
To assess wrist rotation
  Book, spoon, lid on jar, water faucet knob, toy nuts and bolts
To assess stacking
  Blocks, small cars, plates, books
To assess assembling
  Pop beads, Legos, Tinkertoys, beads to string
To assess inserting
  Blocks and container, shape sorter, simple puzzles (one shape to one hole)
  Doll and toy bed, car and toy garage, people figures and toy bus
  Blocks and toy truck
To assess use of index finger to activate toys
  Push-button telephone, buttons and squeakers on Busy-Box, toy piano, or
    computer keyboard
To assess writing
  Paper, chalkboard, chalk, pencil, crayon, felt pen

Gross Motor

To assess standing, walking, climbing, and general play skills
  Child-size chair, rod, hoop
  Low, stable support that is approximately chest height (e.g., low shelf, sofa,
    coffee table)
  Stairs
  Jungle gym, slide, incline, tunnel, barrel, climbing bars

To assess jumping
   Rope, stick
To assess riding
   Riding toy without pedals, tricycle (be sure child's feet reach the pedals)
To assess throwing
   8-inch large ball, Nerf toy, bean bag, cloth block, bucket, target board,
      bowling pins

Adaptive

To assess feeding
   Semi-solid foods such as applesauce and yogurt
   Soft-solid foods such as bananas and soft cookies
   Solid foods such as vegetables, meat, breads, and fruits
   Hard-solid foods such as raw vegetables, apples, and pretzels
   Chewy-solid foods such as meat
   Liquids such as milk, water, and juice
   Cup, spoon, fork, bowls
   Small pitcher or measuring cup with spout
To assess personal hygiene
   Toilet or potty chair
   Soap, water, towel, sink, or washtub
   Toothpaste
   Toothbrush
To assess undressing
   Coat and/or jacket
   Long pants
   Front-fastened and pullover shirts
   Socks
   Shoes
   Hat

Cognitive

To assess sensory processing
   Auditory: rattle, music box, whistle, squeeze-toy
   Visual: colored ball, mobile
   Tactile: soft yarn ball, warm blanket, furry toy
To assess object permanence, causality, and problem solving
   Simple toys (e.g., rattle, bell, squeeze-toy, pinwheel)
   Mechanical toys (e.g., jack-in-the-box, wind-up radio, talking doll)
   Objects with handle or string
   Large push toys (e.g., doll carriage, grocery cart, riding toys)
   Barriers in the environment (e.g., table, chair, shelf, large toy)

To assess categorizing
    Sets of objects to group into categories (e.g., food, clothing, animals,
        transportation)
    Sets of functionally related objects (e.g., baby doll, bottle, blanket; tub, soap,
        washcloth; mirror, brush, comb)
    Sets of objects to group by size, shape, color (e.g., blocks of varying color
        and size, big and little dolls, various red objects)
To assess one-to-one correspondence
    Sets of similar objects (e.g., balls, books)
To assess early literacy
    Cards with environmental signs, logos, labels
    Pictures of familiar people, actions, events
    Pictures and storybooks

Social-Communication

To assess prelinguistic communicative interactions
    Noise-producing objects (e.g., rattle, jingle-bells, squeak-toys)
To assess use of words and word approximations
    Books, picture cards, and common objects and toys

Social

To assess interactions
    Balls, blocks, cars, dress-up clothes, puppets, musical toys, and toy buildings

AEPS™

Fine Motor Area
Birth to Three Years

LIST OF AEPS TEST ITEMS

CAUTION

Quality of movement: Children with cerebral palsy or other motor disorders may exhibit unusual or atypical patterns of movement; for example, the child may move arms or legs stiffly or in an uncoordinated manner, or one arm and/or leg may not be used as well as the other. Referral and consultation with specialists (e.g., occupational therapist, physical therapist) is critical. Scores on the AEPS Test items should reflect poor quality of movement by scoring items either 1 or 0. In addition, a scoring note of Q for Quality of performance should be used to provide the most accurate information about the child's performance. If a child performs skills significantly better with one hand than the other, then scoring each hand individually may be appropriate.

Fine Motor

Reach, Grasp, and Release

STRAND A

GOAL 1 Simultaneously brings hands to midline

CRITERION Child brings hands to the middle of the body at the same time.

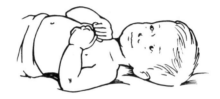

Objective 1.1 Makes directed batting and/or swiping movements with each hand

CRITERION Child bats or swipes at objects with the left and right hand. Child may miss the object. The hand should not be fisted.

Objective 1.2 Makes nondirected movements with each arm

CRITERION Child makes nondirected movements with the left and the right arm when an object is present.

GOAL 2 Brings two objects together at or near midline

CRITERION Child brings two hand-size objects (e.g., block, spoon, rattle) together at or near the middle of the body.

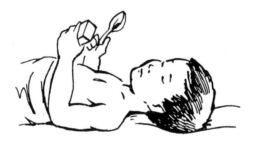

Objective 2.1   **Transfers object from one hand to the other**

CRITERION   Child moves object from one hand to the other hand.

Objective 2.2   **Holds an object in each hand**

CRITERION   Child holds one object in each hand at the same time.

Objective 2.3   **Reaches toward and touches object with each hand**

CRITERION   Child reaches for and touches object with the left hand and the right hand.

GOAL 3   Grasps hand-size object with either hand using ends of thumb, index, and second fingers

CRITERION   Child grasps hand-size object by the fingers so that the pads of the fingers touch the pad of the thumb. Object is not resting in palm.

Fine Motor

Objective 3.1   Grasps hand-size object with either hand using the palm, with object placed toward the thumb and index finger

CRITERION   Child grasps hand-size objects with either hand using the palm. Fingers are closed around object; thumb is rotated toward fingers.

Objective 3.2   Grasps cylindrical object with either hand by closing fingers around it

CRITERION   Child grasps cylindrical object (e.g., crayon, spoon, rattle) with either hand by closing fingers around it.

Objective 3.3   Grasps hand-size object with either hand using whole hand

CRITERION   Child holds object in center of palm with fingers closed around it. Child may use either hand.

GOAL 4   Grasps pea-size object with either hand using tip of the index finger and thumb with hand and/or arm not resting on surface for support

CRITERION   Child grasps pea-size object with hand using tip of the index finger and thumb. Pea-size object (e.g., raisin, Cheerio, small peg) is not held against palm; hand and/or arm is not supported; tip of thumb is rotated toward the index finger.

Objective 4.1   Grasps pea-size object with either hand using tip of the index finger and thumb with hand and/or arm resting on surface for support

CRITERION   Child grasps pea-size object with either hand using tip of index finger and thumb. Pea-size object is not held against palm; the hand and/or arm can rest on surface; tip of thumb is rotated toward the index finger.

Objective 4.2   Grasps pea-size object with either hand using side of the index finger and thumb

CRITERION   Child grasps pea-size object with either hand using side of index finger and thumb. Fingers not used for grasping are held loosely curled but do not flex and extend while grasping.

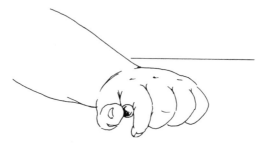

Objective 4.3   Grasps pea-size object with either hand using fingers in a raking and/or scratching movement

CRITERION   Child grasps pea-size object using some or all fingers in a raking and/or scratching movement. The whole arm may move.

GOAL 5 Aligns and stacks objects

CRITERION Child arranges at least three objects (e.g., blocks, cars, plates, stacking rings, books, small chairs) in a line and stacks at least three objects on top of each other.

Objective 5.1 Aligns objects

CRITERION Child arranges at least three objects in a line.

Objective 5.2 Places and releases object balanced on top of another object with either hand

CRITERION Child may use either hand to align, balance, and release object (e.g., a block on another block, a can on another can), without knocking it over.

Objective 5.3 Releases hand-held object onto and/or into a larger target with either hand

CRITERION Child voluntarily releases hand-held object (e.g., a block) onto and/or into a larger target (e.g., a container) with either the left or right hand.

Objective 5.4 Releases hand-held object with each hand

CRITERION Child voluntarily releases hand-held object with the left hand and the right hand.

Fine Motor

Functional Use of Fine Motor Skills

GOAL 1   Rotates either wrist on horizontal plane

CRITERION   Child rotates either wrist to turn and/or twist an object (e.g., removes lid from jar, turns water faucet knob, manipulates toy nuts and bolts).

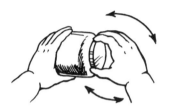

Objective 1.1   Turns object over using wrist and arm rotation with each hand

CRITERION   Child turns wrist and forearm so that the hand is brought from palm down position to palm up position and back again (e.g., brings spoon to mouth, turns page of book). Behavior must be observed with the left hand and the right hand.

GOAL 2   Assembles toy and/or object that require(s) putting pieces together

CRITERION   Child assembles toy and/or object by putting pieces together (e.g., puts top on bottle, puts pop beads together, assembles puzzles).

Objective 2.1   Fits variety of shapes into corresponding spaces

CRITERION   Child completes simple puzzle (one shape to one hole). Adult may point to the corresponding space if necessary.

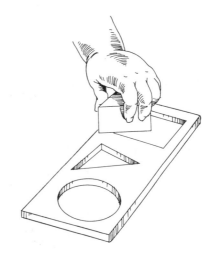

Objective 2.2   Fits object into defined space

CRITERION   Child fits small object into defined space (e.g., puts toy car into garage, puts doll in toy bed, puts people figures into toy bus).

GOAL 3   Uses either index finger to activate objects

CRITERION   Child uses either the left or the right extended index finger to activate objects (e.g., dials telephone, pushes buttons and squeakers on Busy Box, pushes elevator button).

Objective 3.1   Uses either hand to activate objects

CRITERION   Child uses either hand to activate objects (e.g., honks horn, flips light switch, manipulates Busy Box).

Fine Motor

GOAL 4 Orients picture book correctly and turns pages one by one

CRITERION Child holds a picture book with paper pages right side up with the front cover facing upward and turns pages one by one from the beginning of the book to the end.

Objective 4.1 Turns pages of books

CRITERION Child grasps edges of paper book pages and turns without tearing or ripping.

Objective 4.2 Turns/holds picture book right side up

CRITERION Child holds a picture book right side up, turning it if necessary to orient the pictures upright.

GOAL 5 Copies simple written shapes after demonstration

CRITERION Child copies simple written shapes (e.g., cross, square) after demonstration. Shape should resemble the demonstrated model. Any writing implement is acceptable (e.g., chalk, crayon, marker, paintbrush).

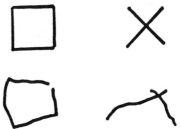

Objective 5.1 Draws circles and lines

CRITERION Child draws circular shapes and makes linear strokes. Lines do not need to be perfectly straight.

Objective 5.2 Scribbles

CRITERION Child scribbles (i.e., makes back-and-forth marks or strokes). Tapping (i.e., dotting motion) with writing implement on paper is not considered scribbling.

AEPS™

Gross Motor Area
Birth to Three Years

LIST OF AEPS TEST ITEMS

Gross Motor

45

3.5   Bears weight on one hand and/or arm while reaching with opposite hand

3.6   Lifts head and chest off surface with weight on arms

Gross Motor

CAUTION

Quality of movement: Children with cerebral palsy or other motor disorders may exhibit unusual or atypical patterns of movement; for example, the child may move arms or legs stiffly or in an uncoordinated manner, or one arm and/or leg may not be used as well as the other. Commonly observed atypical patterns of movement in children with cerebral palsy may include

- Rolling by arching back, throwing head back, retracting arms, and crossing legs

- Moving forward on the stomach using only one arm to pull and one leg to push

- Sitting with rounded back and head resting on shoulders

Referral and consultation with specialists (e.g., occupational therapist, physical therapist) is critical. Scores on the AEPS Test items should reflect the quality of movement by scoring items with either 1 or 0. In addition, a qualifying note of Q for Quality of performance should be used to provide the most accurate information about the child's skill level.

Movement and Locomotion in Supine and Prone Position

GOAL 1 Turns head, moves arms, and kicks legs independently of each other

CRITERION Child moves arms, legs, and head independently of each other when on back. Legs should move alternately.

- Child should not turn head only to one side or to one side consistently more than the other.

- Arms and/or legs should not be stiffly extended.

- Child should not move one arm and/or leg consistently more than the other.

Objective 1.1 Turns head past 45° to the right and left from midline position

CRITERION When on back with the head in midline position, child turns head past 45° to the right and to the left.

- When head turns, child should not assume an asymmetrical tonic neck reflex position (arm toward back of head flexed, arm toward face extended) after 4 months of age.

- Child should not turn head to one side only or turn head to one side consistently more than the other.

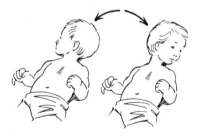

Objective 1.2 Kicks legs

CRITERION When on back, child kicks legs alternately.

- Child should not kick with one leg more vigorously than the other.

- Child should not consistently kick with legs together (e.g., knees touching).

- Legs should not consistently cross during kicking.

Gross Motor

49

Objective 1.3   Waves arms

CRITERION   When on back, child waves arms. Arms should move freely in all directions.

- Child should not consistently move head from side to side when waving arms.

- Hands should not be tightly fisted after 4 months of age.

- Arms should not be stiffly extended.

- Child should not consistently move one arm more than the other.

GOAL 2   Rolls by turning segmentally from stomach to back and from back to stomach

CRITERION   Child rolls by shifting weight to one side of the body, leading with head, shoulder, or hip.

- Child should not arch back or throw head backward when rolling.

- Legs should not cross while child is rolling.

- Child should not consistently catch arm under trunk after rolling from back.

- Child should not roll in one direction only.

Objective 2.1   Rolls from back to stomach

CRITERION   Child rolls from back to stomach by shifting weight to one side of the body, leading with head, shoulder, or hip.

- Child should not arch back or throw head backward when rolling.

- Legs should not cross while child is rolling.

- Child should not consistently catch arm under trunk after rolling from back.

- Child should not roll in one direction only.

Objective 2.2   Rolls from stomach to back

CRITERION   Child rolls from stomach to back by shifting weight to one side of the body leading with head, shoulder, or hip.

- When attempting to roll, child should not arch back and neck with arms held at sides.

- Child should not roll in one direction only.

- Child should not cross legs while rolling.

GOAL 3   Creeps forward using alternating arm
and leg movements

CRITERION   Child moves forward at least 6 feet on hands and
knees. Child bears weight on hands and knees and
moves one arm and opposite leg, then other arm and
opposite leg. Stomach remains lifted off surface.

Objective 3.1   **Rocks while in a creeping position**

CRITERION   While in a creeping position (both hands and knees
on surface, stomach lifted off surface), child rocks
back and forth at least two consecutive times.

Objective 3.2   Assumes creeping position

> CRITERION   Child assumes creeping position with both hands and knees on surface and stomach lifted off surface.

Objective 3.3   Crawls forward on stomach

> CRITERION   Child moves forward with stomach touching the surface, pulling with both arms, and supporting weight on hands and/or arms. Legs alternately bend and straighten, but do not cross, as child moves forward at least 2 feet.

Objective 3.4   Pivots on stomach

> CRITERION   Child pivots 180° in each direction in a semi-circle when on stomach.

Gross Motor

Objective 3.5   **Bears weight on one hand and/or arm while reaching with opposite hand**

> CRITERION   When on stomach, child bears weight on one hand and/or arm while reaching with opposite hand. Behavior must be observed with each hand.

Objective 3.6   **Lifts head and chest off surface with weight on arms**

> CRITERION   Child lifts head and chest off surface, with weight on bent or straight arms, keeping head in midline. Knees and legs should not be crossed.

Balance in Sitting

GOAL 1   Assumes balanced sitting position

CRITERION   From any position (e.g., standing, creeping, lying down), the child moves to a sitting position on a flat surface without support.

Note   *A child should not be placed in or encouraged to use a "W" sitting position (e.g., child's buttocks on floor between legs).*

Objective 1.1   Assumes hands and knees position from sitting

CRITERION   From a sitting position, child moves to a hands and knees position using body rotation (i.e., reaches across the body with either the right or left arm and shifts weight to knees).

Objective 1.2   Regains balanced, upright sitting position after reaching across the body to the right and to the left

CRITERION   When sitting, child regains a balanced, upright sitting position after reaching across the body to the right and to the left.

- Child should not regain balanced, upright sitting position from one side better than the other.

- When regaining sitting position, child's hands should not fist on either side.

Objective 1.3   Regains balanced, upright sitting position after leaning to the left, to the right, and forward

CRITERION   When sitting, child regains a balanced, upright sitting position after leaning to the left, to the right, and forward.

- Child should not regain a balanced, upright sitting position from one side better than the other.

- When regaining sitting position, child's hands should not fist on either side.

Objective 1.4   Sits balanced without support

CRITERION   Child sits in a balanced position with back straight and hands not touching the surface for at least 30 seconds.

Objective 1.5   Sits balanced using hands for support

CRITERION   When placed in sitting position, child balances using hands for support and holding head in midline for at least 60 seconds.

Objective 1.6   Holds head in midline when in supported sitting position

CRITERION   When sitting in a supported position, child holds head in midline for at least 30 seconds. Child should not consistently sit with back rounded.

GOAL 2 Sits down in and gets out of chair

CRITERION Child maneuvers self to sit down in and get out of child-size chair.

Objective 2.1 Sits down in chair

CRITERION Child maneuvers self to sit down in child-size chair.

Objective 2.2 Maintains a sitting position in chair

CRITERION Child maintains unsupported, balanced sitting position in child-size chair.

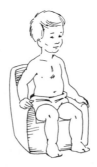

Gross Motor

STRAND C

Balance and Mobility

GOAL 1 Walks avoiding obstacles

CRITERION When walking unsupported, child moves to avoid obstacles (e.g., toys, furniture, people).

Objective 1.1 Walks without support

CRITERION Child walks unsupported for at least 6 feet. Child's head is erect and in midline, and back is straight.

Objective 1.2 Walks with one-hand support

CRITERION Child walks forward at least 15 feet when holding onto support with one hand. Child's head is erect and in midline, and back is straight.

Objective 1.3 Walks with two-hand support

CRITERION Child walks forward at least 15 feet when holding onto support with two hands. Child's head is erect and in midline, and back is straight. Child bends one knee and lifts foot off the ground, placing it next to and in front of the opposite foot. Opposite foot remains slightly bent and in contact with the floor.

Objective 1.4   Stands unsupported

CRITERION   Child stands unsupported for at least 30 seconds. Child's head is erect and in midline, and back is straight. Knees are slightly bent and feet are directly under hips and flat on floor.

Objective 1.5   Cruises

CRITERION   Child cruises (side-steps) at least 3 feet to the left and to the right, holding onto a stable support that is approximately chest height. Child's head is erect and in midline, and back is straight.

GOAL 2   Stoops and regains balanced standing position without support

CRITERION   After stooping or squatting, child regains a balanced standing position without using a support or sitting down.

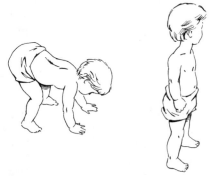

Objective 2.1   Rises from sitting position to standing position

CRITERION   Child rises from a sitting position to a standing position without support.

Gross Motor

Objective 2.2   Pulls to standing position

> CRITERION   Child pulls to standing position from sitting, kneeling, and/or creeping position using support.

Objective 2.3   Pulls to kneeling position

> CRITERION   Child pulls to a kneeling position from a sitting and/or creeping position by holding onto support with both hands. Child moves one knee close to the support, then the other knee.

GOAL 3   Runs avoiding obstacles

> CRITERION   Child avoids obstacles when running.

Objective 3.1   Runs

> CRITERION   Child runs smoothly. Child's trunk is inclined slightly forward, arms swing freely, and there is a momentary period where there is no support by either leg.

Objective 3.2   Walks fast

> CRITERION   Child walks fast. Motion differs from a run in that the body appears stiff (i.e., knees flex only slightly and one foot is always on floor).

GOAL 4   Walks up and down stairs

> CRITERION   Child walks up and down stairs, holding or not holding rail or wall with one hand, alternating or not alternating feet.

Objective 4.1   Walks up and down stairs using two-hand support

CRITERION   Child walks up and down stairs using two-hand support (e.g., holding railings, holding adult's hands), alternating or not alternating feet.

Objective 4.2   Moves up and down stairs

CRITERION   Child creeps, crawls, and/or scoots on buttocks up and down stairs.

Objective 4.3   Gets up and down from low structure

CRITERION   Child climbs onto and gets off a low, stable structure (e.g., low step, raised platform).

Gross Motor

STRAND
D

Play Skills

GOAL 1   Jumps forward

CRITERION   Child jumps forward with feet together (e.g., child jumps over rope, stick, chalk line).

Objective 1.1   **Jumps up**

CRITERION   Child jumps up with feet together.

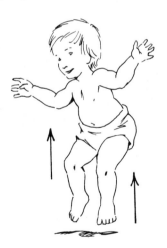

Objective 1.2   **Jumps from low structure**

CRITERION   Child jumps from a low, stable structure (e.g., low step, raised platform, curb) to a supporting surface. Feet do not have to land together.

GOAL 2   Pedals and steers tricycle

CRITERION   When sitting on a tricycle with feet on pedals, child pedals and steers tricycle forward for at least 5 feet.

Objective 2.1   Pushes riding toy with feet while steering

CRITERION   When sitting on a riding toy with feet on surface, child pushes with feet while steering for at least 5 feet.

Objective 2.2   Sits on riding toy or in wagon while adult pushes

CRITERION   Child maintains balanced sitting position on riding toy or in wagon without support while adult steers and pushes toy or pulls wagon for at least 5 feet.

GOAL 3   Catches, kicks, throws, and rolls ball or similar object

CRITERION   Child performs the following play skills:

- Catches ball or similar object

- Kicks ball or similar object

- Throws ball or similar object at target

- Rolls ball at target

Note   *Child must score a 2 in Objective 3.1 through Objective 3.4 in order to score a 2 on Goal 3. If the child scores a 1 and/or a 0 on some objectives, then Goal 3 should be scored as a 1. If the child scores a 0 on all objectives, then Goal 3 should be scored as a 0.*

Objective 3.1   Catches ball or similar object

CRITERION   When a large object is tossed to child, child catches the object with two hands. Child can be in any position that is functional for the child.

Objective 3.2   Kicks ball or similar object

CRITERION   While standing and when object is in front of child's feet, child kicks object forward with one foot while maintaining balance.

Objective 3.3   Throws ball or similar object at target

CRITERION   In any position that is functional, child throws object forward with one or two hands within 18 inches of target. Object can be thrown overhand or underhand.

Objective 3.4   Rolls ball at target

CRITERION   In any position that is functional, child rolls ball with one or two hands within 18 inches of target.

GOAL 4   Climbs up and down play equipment

CRITERION   Child climbs up and down ladders; moves up and down inclines; and moves under, over, and through obstacles (e.g., child climbs on jungle gym or slide; walks up and down incline; navigates through obstacle course, tunnel, or barrel).

Objective 4.1   **Moves up and down inclines**

CRITERION   Child moves up and down inclines (e.g., child climbs up and slides down slide, walks and/or crawls up ramp).

Objective 4.2   **Moves under, over, and through obstacles**

CRITERION   Child moves under, over, and through obstacles (e.g., child crawls under table, moves through barrels or tunnels, climbs into and out of sandbox).

AEPS™

Adaptive Area
Birth to Three Years

LIST OF AEPS TEST ITEMS

Adaptive

1.3 Takes off pants

1.4 Takes off socks

1.5 Takes off shoes

1.6 Takes off hat

NOTE

Several factors should be considered when administering the Adaptive Area. Parental and cultural values have an effect on what skills a child learns and in what order the skills are learned. Toilet training, the introduction of food and feeding implements, and the degree of personal cleanliness are examples of behaviors that differ across cultures and families. The examiner needs to be sensitive to culturally determined limits and individual family preferences when assessing a child's performance on adaptive items.

The child should use actions (eating with a spoon rather than fingers) and materials (wiping nose with a tissue rather than a sleeve) that are as socially acceptable as possible for the child's developmental age. The lack of socially acceptable skills often results in the exclusion of the child from certain settings. For this reason, the examiner should consider this performance dimension when assessing a child.

For feeding, the child should be in a position so that functioning of the oral mechanism (mouth, teeth, tongue, jaws, throat) is maximized. Different positions may need to be tried before a suitable one is found. The interventionist should consider the following factors when positioning the child:

1. The child should be as upright as possible (e.g., on a prone or supine board, propped on a wedge, seated in a chair). If seated, then the child's legs should be bent at the hips, knees, and ankles with feet on a solid surface (e.g., floor).

2. The child's head should be in midline and upright, not resting on the child's chest or tilted back.

3. The child should be comfortable and relaxed.

4. The child's spine should be straight, not curved to the side or forward.

5. The child should be able to maintain the position for the entire meal.

6. The child's arms and hands should be free to move.

7. The food should be visible to the child. If the child self-feeds, then the food should be within easy reach of the child.

Adaptive

CAUTION

If a child consistently demonstrates any of the following behaviors, evaluation by a physical or occupational therapist is warranted.

- Lip retraction (lips pulled tightly back)
- Lip pursing (lips tightly puckering)
- Tongue thrust (forceful protrusion of tongue)
- Tongue held far back in the mouth or pressed hard up against roof of mouth
- Persistent suckle (snake-like action of the tongue in and out of mouth).
- Tonic-bite reflex (strong closing of jaws with difficulty re-opening)
- Jaw thrust (strong downward opening of jaw)

Feeding

GOAL 1 Uses tongue and lips to take in and swallow solid foods and liquids

CRITERION   Child takes in and swallows liquids and solid foods without choking or gagging. Child uses a suck and active lip movement with liquids. Child eats a variety of foods and liquids appropriate for the age of the child: semi-solid foods such as applesauce and yogurt; solid foods such as vegetables, meat, breads, and fruits; liquids such as milk, water, and juice.

Note   *Child must score a 2 on Objective 1.1 through Objective 1.4 in order to score a 2 on Goal 1. If the child scores a 1 and/or a 0 on some objectives, then Goal 1 should be scored as a 1. If the child scores a 0 on all objectives, then Goal 1 should be scored with a 0.*

Objective 1.1 Uses lips to take in liquids from a cup and/or glass

CRITERION   Child drinks liquid from a cup and/or glass using lips to seal the cup rim, draw in liquid, and retain liquid in mouth when swallowing.

Objective 1.2 Uses lips to take food off spoon and/or fork

CRITERION   Child takes food (e.g., yogurt, applesauce, soft vegetables) off a utensil using upper lip movement to clean utensil as it is removed from the mouth. The utensil is not scraped on child's upper or lower lip.

Objective 1.3 Swallows solid and semi-solid foods

CRITERION   Child swallows soft, hard, chewy, and semi-solid bites of food without gagging, choking, or swallowing pieces whole, including

- Soft solids: bananas and soft cookies
- Hard solids: raw vegetables, apples, and pretzels
- Chewy solids: meats and dried fruits
- Semi-solids: applesauce and yogurt

Objective 1.4 Swallows liquids

CRITERION   Child swallows liquid from a bottle, breast, or cup without choking or gagging while in a semi-reclining or upright position, with minimal loss of liquid from mouth.

GOAL 2   Bites and chews hard and chewy foods

CRITERION   Child uses teeth to bite through and chew hard foods (e.g., apples, raw vegetables, pretzels) and chewy foods (e.g., meats, dried fruits). The tongue moves the food from side to side within the mouth as the jaw moves up, down, and diagonally to break up the food. Child should not

- Break up or rip off pieces of food between lips

- Use munching pattern (up-and-down jaw movements without side-to-side tongue movement)

- Show excessive protrusion or lateral deviation of jaw

Objective 2.1   Bites and chews soft and crisp foods

CRITERION   Child uses teeth or gums to bite through and chew soft foods (e.g., bananas, cooked vegetables, macaroni) and crisp foods (e.g., crackers, cookies). The tongue moves the food from side to side within the mouth as the jaw moves up, down, and diagonally to break up the food.

Objective 2.2   Munches soft and crisp foods

CRITERION   Child breaks up soft and crisp foods by using a simple munching pattern. Child appears to smack and/or suck food while opening and closing mouth. The jaw moves up and down. Food may not be transferred from one side of mouth to the other.

GOAL 3   Drinks from cup and/or glass

CRITERION   Child drinks from a cup and/or glass by bringing cup to mouth and returns cup to surface without spilling.

Objective 3.1   Drinks from cup and/or glass with some spilling

CRITERION   Child brings cup and/or glass to mouth and drinks with minimal spilling. Child may release cup before returning to surface.

Objective 3.2   Drinks from cup and/or glass held by adult

CRITERION   Child sucks and swallows liquid from a cup and/or glass held by an adult. Child uses some lip closure on rim of cup. Some loss of liquid may occur.

GOAL 4   Eats with fork and/or spoon

CRITERION   Child eats with fork and/or spoon by spearing or scooping food and bringing it to mouth with minimal spilling.

Objective 4.1   Brings food to mouth using utensil

CRITERION   Child eats with fork and/or spoon by bringing filled utensil to mouth. Some spilling may occur; child may have assistance filling utensil.

Objective 4.2   Eats with fingers

CRITERION   Child eats with fingers by grasping and bringing to mouth large and/or small pieces of food.

Objective 4.3   Accepts food presented on spoon

CRITERION   When offered food from a spoon, child opens mouth and closes jaw and lips around the utensil to take in semi-solid foods (e.g., applesauce, yogurt).

GOAL 5   Transfers food and liquid between containers

CRITERION   Child scoops food and pours liquid from one container to another without spilling. Present child with an amount of liquid that will not overfill the container.

Objective 5.1   Pours liquid between containers

CRITERION   When presented with an amount of liquid that will not overfill the container, the child pours liquid from one container into another without spilling.

Objective 5.2   Transfers food between containers

CRITERION   Child uses utensil to scoop and transfer food from one container to another.

Adaptive

Personal Hygiene

GOAL 1   Initiates toileting

CRITERION   Child initiates toileting and demonstrates bowel and bladder control. Child may need help completing toileting routine. Occasional reminders are acceptable.

Objective 1.1   Demonstrates bowel and bladder control

CRITERION   Child demonstrates bowel and bladder control when taken to the toilet on a regular basis. Occasional accidents are acceptable.

Objective 1.2   Indicates awareness of soiled and wet pants and/or diapers

CRITERION   Child indicates awareness of soiled and wet pants and/or diapers by verbalizing, gesturing, and/or signing.

GOAL 2   Washes and dries hands

CRITERION   Child completes hand washing and drying routine by turning faucet on and off, washing with soap, drying hands, and returning towel to towel rack or throwing paper towel away. Child may request assistance in turning faucet on and off.

Objective 2.1   Washes hands

CRITERION   Child washes hands with soap and rinses with water. Adult may turn faucet on and off.

GOAL 3   Brushes teeth

CRITERION   After adult puts toothpaste on toothbrush, child brushes teeth. Adult may provide assistance to effectively clean teeth.

Objective 3.1   Cooperates with teeth brushing

CRITERION   Child opens mouth and allows teeth to be brushed long enough to effectively clean teeth.

Undressing

GOAL 1   Undresses self

CRITERION   Child uses any functional means to perform all of the following undressing activities:

- Takes off pullover shirt/sweater
- Takes off front-fastened coat, jacket, or shirt (adult may assist in unfastening)
- Takes off long pants from both feet (adult may assist in unfastening)
- Takes off socks
- Takes off shoes (adult may assist in unfastening)
- Takes off hat (adult may assist in unfastening)

Children may display greater skill with one garment than another garment of the same type (e.g., two different pullover shirts) due to the fit. In such cases, this inconsistency of skill performance should be noted by scoring items as 1.

Note   *Child must score a 2 on Objective 1.1 through Objective 1.6 in order to score a 2 on Goal 1. If the child scores a 1 and/or a 0 on some objectives, then Goal 1 should be scored as a 1. If the child scores a 0 on all objectives, then Goal 1 should be scored with a 0.*

Objective 1.1   Takes off pullover shirt/sweater

CRITERION   Child uses any functional means to take off pullover shirt or sweater.

Objective 1.2   Takes off front-fastened coat, jacket, or shirt

CRITERION   Child uses any functional means to take off front-fastened coat and/or shirt. Adult may assist in unfastening.

Objective 1.3   Takes off pants

CRITERION   Child uses any functional means to take off long pants from both feet. Adult may assist in unfastening.

Adaptive

Objective 1.4   Takes off socks

CRITERION   Child uses any functional means to take off socks.

Objective 1.5   Takes off shoes

CRITERION   Child uses any functional means to take off shoes. Adult may assist in unfastening.

Objective 1.6   Takes off hat

CRITERION   Child uses any functional means to take off hat. Adult may assist in unfastening.

AEPS™

Cognitive Area
Birth to Three Years

LIST OF AEPS TEST ITEMS

G2 Locates object in latter of two successive hiding places 83

2.1 Locates object and/or person hidden while child is watching

2.2 Locates object and/or person who is partially hidden while child is watching

2.3 Reacts when object and/or person hides from view

G3 Maintains search for object that is not in its usual location 84

3.1 Looks for object in usual location

C Causality 85

G1 Correctly activates mechanical toy .85

1.1 Correctly activates simple toy

1.2 Acts on mechanical and/or simple toy in some way

1.3 Indicates interest in simple and/or mechanical toy

G2 Reproduces part of interactive game and/or action in order to continue game and/or action 85

2.1 Indicates desire to continue familiar game and/or action

D Imitation 86

G1 Imitates motor action that is not commonly used 86

1.1 Imitates motor action that is commonly used

G2   **Imitates words that are not frequently used** 86

2.1   Imitates speech sounds that are not frequently used

2.2   Imitates words that are frequently used

E   Problem Solving 87

G1   **Retains objects when new object is obtained** 87

1.1   Retains one object when second object is obtained

1.2   Retains object

G2   **Uses an object to obtain another object** 87

2.1   Uses part of object and/or support to obtain another object

G3   **Navigates large object around barriers** 87

3.1   Moves barrier or goes around barrier to obtain object

3.2   Moves around barrier to change location

G4   **Solves common problems** 88

4.1   Uses more than one strategy in attempt to solve common problem

---

F   Interaction with Objects 89

G1   **Uses imaginary objects in play** 89

1.1   Uses representational actions with objects

1.2   Uses functionally appropriate actions with objects

Cognitive

G6 Repeats simple nursery rhymes 93

6.1 Fills in rhyming words in familiar rhymes

6.2 Says nursery rhymes along with familiar adult

CAUTION

When administering this area, the examiner should be aware that gross and fine motor abilities may affect the child's performance of cognitive skills; for example, activation of a mechanical toy requires fine motor abilities as well as the concept of causality.

Cognitive

STRAND A

Sensory Stimuli

GOAL 1   Orients to auditory, visual, and tactile events

CRITERION   Child orients to (i.e., turns, looks, reaches, moves toward) auditory, visual, and tactile events when presented a variety of sensory stimuli:

- Auditory: person vocalizing, rattle, music box, whistle, squeeze-toy

- Visual: person smiling, colored ball, mobile

- Tactile: soft yarn ball, warm blanket, furry stuffed toy

Note   *Child must score a 2 in Objective 1.1 through Objective 1.4 in order to score a 2 on Goal 1. If the child scores a 1 and/or a 0 on some objectives, then Goal 1 should be scored as a 1. If the child scores a 0 on all objectives, then Goal 1 should be scored as a 0.*

Objective 1.1   Orients to auditory events

CRITERION   Child orients to sound (nonvocal or vocal) by turning, looking, reaching, and/or moving in the direction of the sound.

Objective 1.2   Orients to visual events

CRITERION   Child orients to visual events by turning, looking, reaching, and/or moving in direction of source that is within child's visual field.

Objective 1.3   Orients to tactile stimulation

CRITERION   Child orients to tactile stimulation (e.g., soft yarn ball, warm blanket, furry stuffed toy) by turning, looking, reaching, and/or moving in direction of source.

Objective 1.4   Responds to auditory, visual, and tactile events

CRITERION   Child responds by ceasing or increasing activity momentarily when presented with auditory, visual, and tactile events:

- Auditory: person vocalizing, rattle, music box, whistle, squeeze-toy

- Visual: person smiling, colored ball, mobile

- Tactile: soft yarn ball, warm blanket, furry stuffed toy

Object Permanence

GOAL 1 Visually follows object and/or person to point of disappearance

CRITERION Child moves eyes and/or head to visually follow object or person to point of disappearance.

Objective 1.1 Visually follows object moving in horizontal, vertical, and circular directions

CRITERION Child visually follows object moving in horizontal, vertical, and circular directions. Situations in the environment may include

- Horizontal: watches ball roll across visual field

- Vertical: watches ball thrown up and coming back down

- Circular: watches toy ferris wheel turn around, balloon floating

Objective 1.2 Focuses on object and/or person

CRITERION Child visually focuses for at least 4 seconds on a stationary object and/or person within child's visual field.

GOAL 2 Locates object in latter of two successive hiding places

CRITERION After child sees object hidden first in one place, then in another, child immediately finds hidden object in second place (e.g., adult hides toy interesting to the child in one cup and then moves toy to another cup before child is allowed to retrieve it; child finds toy by looking only in second cup).

Objective 2.1 Locates object and/or person hidden while child is watching

CRITERION After child sees object and/or person hidden, child immediately finds hidden object and/or person (e.g., people hiding as part of Hide-and-Seek, ball rolling under a table, crayon hidden under paper).

Cognitive

Objective 2.2   **Locates object and/or person who is partially hidden while child is watching**

CRITERION   After child sees object and/or person partially hidden, child immediately finds hidden object and/or person (e.g., child retrieves teddy bear that has been partially hidden under the bedcovers or a toy car that has been partially parked inside a block structure).

Objective 2.3   **Reacts when object and/or person hides from view**

CRITERION   Child reacts in some way when object and/or person disappears from view. Child does not have to indicate location of hidden object and/or person. Reactions may include momentary staring, crying, obvious expressions of surprise, and/or head turning.

GOAL 3   **Maintains search for object that is not in its usual location**

CRITERION   Child continues to search for an object in more than one place when it is not found in its usual location (e.g., when coat is not in coat closet, child will look in several other likely places).

Objective 3.1   **Looks for object in usual location**

CRITERION   Child looks for an object in its usual location (e.g., child looks in toy box for favorite toy, goes to coat closet or rack for coat).

STRAND C

Causality

GOAL 1 Correctly activates mechanical toy

CRITERION   Child correctly activates mechanical toy (e.g., jack-in-the-box, wind-up radio, talking doll, See-N-Say; child winds up dial on toy radio, pulls lever on toy cash register). Demonstrate the toy's action if necessary.

Objective 1.1 Correctly activates simple toy

CRITERION   Child correctly activates simple toy (e.g., rattle, bell, squeeze-toy, pinwheel). Demonstrate the toy's action if necessary.

Objective 1.2 Acts on mechanical and/or simple toy in some way

CRITERION   Child acts on mechanical and/or simple toy in some way (e.g., hits, touches, pushes), causing it to move or make a noise (e.g., shakes a squeeze-toy, hits a wind-up radio). Child's action is not appropriate for activating the object.

Objective 1.3 Indicates interest in simple and/or mechanical toy

CRITERION   When simple and/or mechanical toy is activated, child waves arms, vocalizes, laughs, smiles, kicks legs, stares, and/or ceases activity.

GOAL 2 Reproduces part of interactive game and/or action in order to continue game and/or action

CRITERION   Child indicates desire to continue interactive game and/or action (e.g., Pat-a-cake, Peekaboo) by performing an action that is part of game (e.g., child claps hands, covers eyes when adult pauses during game).

Objective 2.1 Indicates desire to continue familiar game and/or action

CRITERION   Child indicates desire to continue familiar game and/or action (e.g., Peekaboo; child waves arms, bounces, vocalizes, laughs, smiles, kicks legs).

Cognitive

Imitation

GOAL 1   Imitates motor action that is not commonly used

CRITERION   Child imitates motor action that is not commonly used (e.g., pats knee, taps foot). The action should not be part of familiar songs and/or activities. Action should be appropriate for child's motor abilities.

Objective 1.1   Imitates motor action that is commonly used

CRITERION   Child imitates motor action that is commonly used (e.g., claps hands in front of self, pats table). Commonly used motor actions are those that the child has previously produced.

GOAL 2   Imitates words that are not frequently used

CRITERION   Child imitates words that he or she does not frequently use.

Objective 2.1   Imitates speech sounds that are not frequently used

CRITERION   Child imitates developmentally appropriate speech sounds that he or she does not frequently use.

Objective 2.2   Imitates words that are frequently used

CRITERION   Child imitates words that he or she frequently uses.

Problem Solving

GOAL 1   Retains objects when new object is obtained

CRITERION   Child uses any means to retain objects that he or she is using when new object is acquired (e.g., child holds several objects in one hand; puts objects into container or pocket; puts some items in mouth, on lap, under arm, between legs).

Objective 1.1   Retains one object when second object is obtained

CRITERION   Child uses any means to retain one object when a second one is obtained (e.g., child holds cookie in one hand and obtains second cookie with the other hand).

Objective 1.2   Retains object

CRITERION   Child uses any means to retain an object (e.g., child grasps object with fingers, holds in palm of hand, grips between both hands, presses between forearm and torso).

GOAL 2   Uses an object to obtain another object

CRITERION   Child moves or manipulates an object to obtain another object (e.g., child moves a stool to reach an object placed out of reach, uses a stick to obtain object out of reach across the table).

Objective 2.1   Uses part of object and/or support to obtain another object

CRITERION   Child obtains object by pulling on part of the object (e.g., handle, attached string) and/or by pulling support on which object is resting (e.g., tray, placemat, blanket).

GOAL 3   Navigates large object around barriers

CRITERION   Child moves large object around barriers (e.g., child moves toy grocery cart, doll carriage, riding toy around furniture).

Objective 3.1   **Moves barrier or goes around barrier to obtain object**

CRITERION   Child moves barrier or goes around barrier (e.g., table, chair, large toy) to obtain an object.

Objective 3.2   **Moves around barrier to change location**

CRITERION   Child moves around barrier to change location.

GOAL 4   Solves common problems

CRITERION   Child uses different strategies to solve common problems (e.g., when child wants an object that is out of reach, child calls to an adult and then gets a chair to stand on when adult does not respond).

Objective 4.1   **Uses more than one strategy in attempt to solve common problem**

CRITERION   Child attempts to solve problems by using more than one strategy (e.g., when working a puzzle, child turns one piece around and then tries another puzzle piece when the first one does not fit; when child wants a toy from high shelf, child reaches for toy, then attempts to knock it down with another object; when presented with food that is in a jar with a tight lid, the child attempts to open the jar by turning the lid, then tries banging the jar on the table).

Interaction with Objects

GOAL 1   Uses imaginary objects in play

CRITERION   Child uses imaginary objects in play. Imaginary play consists of child pretending and/or imagining that an object and/or event is occurring (e.g., child pretends to climb a mountain in a classroom, go to outer space in a cardboard box, have lions and tigers in cages when pretending to visit the zoo).

Objective 1.1   Uses representational actions with objects

CRITERION   Child uses one object to represent another (e.g., child uses a box as a hat, a spoon as a telephone, a stick to stir food).

Objective 1.2   Uses functionally appropriate actions with objects

CRITERION   Child acts on objects using functionally or socially appropriate actions. Functionally or socially appropriate actions are those for which the object was intended or designed (e.g., child holds play telephone to ear, puts comb to head and attempts to comb hair, puts glasses on eyes).

Objective 1.3   Uses simple motor actions on different objects

CRITERION   Child acts on objects using simple motor actions (e.g., mouths, pats, bangs, shakes, rubs). Simple motor actions are any group of actions used on objects irrespective of the physical characteristics of the objects (e.g., when given a rattle, a small squeeze-toy, or a cloth book, the child bangs, shakes, and mouths all objects in a similar fashion).

Objective 1.4   Uses sensory examination with objects

CRITERION   Child acts on objects using sensory examination (e.g., child looks at, manipulates, listens to, sniffs, and mouths objects). Sensory examination includes the use of any sense (e.g., visual, auditory, tactile, olfactory, gustatory) that allows the child to gain information about an object.

Cognitive

Early Concepts

GOAL 1 Categorizes like objects

CRITERION Child puts together at least three objects in a group according to a broad-based category (e.g., food, clothing, animals; child gathers all toy animals together, puts play dishes and utensils on table, gathers clothing in order to play dress-up).

Objective 1.1 Groups functionally related objects

CRITERION Child puts together at least three objects that are conventionally or functionally related (e.g., during pretend play, child collects doll, bottle, and blanket together; while playing in the sandbox, child gets bucket, shovel, and sifter).

Objective 1.2 Groups objects according to size, shape, and/or color

CRITERION Child groups objects according to size, shape, and/or color when provided with a visual model (e.g., large versus small; circles, triangles, squares; blue, red, green; child follows directions to "Put all the big blocks in this box" or "Keep all the red cups together," when shown big blocks and red cups).

Objective 1.3 Matches pictures and/or objects

CRITERION When given three to four different pictures and/or objects, child picks up or points to a matching picture and/or matching object (e.g., child correctly matches toys to pictures of stuffed animals, dishes, and blocks on toy shelves when picking up).

GOAL 2 Demonstrates functional use of one-to-one correspondence

CRITERION Child demonstrates one-to-one correspondence by assigning one object to each of two or more objects and/or people (e.g., child places one fork next to each plate, gives one paintbrush to each child).

Objective 2.1 Demonstrates concept of one

CRITERION When presented with several like objects and asked to indicate one, child shows, gives, and/or assigns one and only one object (e.g., child takes one crayon when offered a box with several crayons and asked to "Just take one crayon").

GOAL 3 Recognizes environmental symbols (signs, logos, labels)

CRITERION Child assigns correct meaning and words to familiar symbols such as road signs, logos for brand names, restaurants, stores, and familiar food and product labels by producing an associated word or action (e.g., child says, "I want hamburger" at the sight of a fast-food logo, says, "Bus" at the bus stop sign, shows his or her shoes at the sight of a matching logo).

Objective 3.1 Labels familiar people, actions, objects, and events in pictures

CRITERION Child uses words or word approximations in any language (including sign language) to correctly label pictures of familiar objects, actions, people, and events.

GOAL 4 Demonstrates functional use of reading materials

CRITERION Child demonstrates functional use of reading materials (e.g., storybooks, magazines, phone/address books, menus, newspapers). Child shows an awareness that text contains a message by using reading behaviors with books. The child is not actually reading but is using printed materials in a functional and appropriate fashion (e.g., child "reads" a story to an adult using narration based on pictures, looks at a menu and decides to eat spaghetti, assigns prices to products while looking at advertisements; the child is not actually reading but is using reading behaviors appropriately).

Objective 4.1 Orally fills in or completes familiar text while looking at picture books

CRITERION Child fills in the correct words if an adult leaves out words while reading out loud (e.g., adult reads "Goodnight house; goodnight _____", and the child fills in the word "mouse").

Cognitive

Objective 4.2   Makes comments and asks questions while looking at picture books

CRITERION   Child uses gestures and/or words to share or obtain information about pictures and text in familiar books (e.g., the child looks at the page intently while asking, "Where's the mouse?" and then points to the mouse picture on the page and says, "There it is!").

Objective 4.3   Sits and attends to entire story during shared reading time

CRITERION   Child sits close to adult and attends while the adult reads an entire short children's book.

Note   *For children from cultures with oral rather than literate traditions, Objectives 4.2 and 4.3 can be modified by substituting oral stories for books, storytelling for reading, spoken words for text, and so forth.*

GOAL 5   Demonstrates use of common opposite concepts

CRITERION   Child demonstrates understanding of at least six pairs of early opposite concepts by sorting, labeling, or selecting objects with the appropriate quality from at least six pairs (e.g., child takes the correct paper when an adult presents piles of large- and small-size paper; child answers correctly when asked if pants are wet or dry; child complies with request to take book off top shelf when there are books on all shelves). Examples of opposite concepts may include but are not limited to the following:

| big/little | hot/cold | wet/dry | up/down | fast/slow |
| top/bottom | in/out | full/empty | stop/go | clean/dirty |

Objective 5.1   Demonstrates use of at least four pairs of common opposite concepts

CRITERION   Child demonstrates understanding of early opposite concepts by showing, sorting, labeling, or selecting the appropriate qualities. See previous examples.

Objective 5.2   Demonstrates use of at least two pairs of common opposite concepts

CRITERION   Child demonstrates understanding of early opposite concepts by showing, sorting, labeling, or selecting the appropriate qualities. See previous examples.

GOAL 6 Repeats simple nursery rhymes

CRITERION Child repeats at least two lines of simple nursery rhymes or songs without prompts (e.g., "Humpty Dumpty sat on a wall; Humpty Dumpty had a great fall"; "Baa baa black sheep, have you any wool? Yes, sir, yes, sir, three bags full"; "Three little monkeys jumping on the bed. One fell off and bumped his head"). The rhymes should be familiar and simple. Child does not have to remember the entire rhyme. Child can make minor mistakes in reciting non-rhyming words.

Objective 6.1 Fills in rhyming words in familiar rhymes

CRITERION Child fills in the appropriate word in a familiar nursery rhyme when adult recites the entire rhyme except for the one rhyming word (e.g., The adult says, "I'm a little teapot short and stout. Tip me over and pour me _____," and the child says, "out").

Objective 6.2 Says nursery rhymes along with familiar adult

CRITERION Child shows recognition of sound games by joining in with adult or other children reciting nursery rhymes, keeping the pace and intonation of the rhyme and emphasizing the main ideas, nouns, and rhyming words (e.g., while the group sings "Itsy, Bitsy Spider," the child clearly says key words such as "spider," "spout," "down," "rain," "out," with special emphasis on "spout" and "out").

Cognitive

AEPS™

Social-Communication Area
Birth to Three Years

LIST OF AEPS TEST ITEMS

Social-Communication

95

1.2 Points to an object, person, and/or event

1.3 Gestures and/or vocalizes to greet others

1.4 Uses gestures and/or vocalizations to protest actions and/or reject objects or people

2.1 Uses consistent consonant–vowel combinations

2.2 Uses nonspecific consonant–vowel combinations and/or jargon

2.3 Vocalizes to express affective states

2.4 Vocalizes open syllables

C Comprehension of Words and Sentences . . . 103

1.1 Locates common objects, people, and/or events in unfamiliar pictures

1.2 Locates common objects, people, and/or events in familiar pictures

1.3 Locates common objects, people, and/or events with contextual cues

1.4 Recognizes own name

1.5 Quiets to familiar voice

2.1 Carries out two-step direction with contextual cues

2.2 Carries out one-step direction without contextual cues

2.3 Carries out one-step direction with contextual cues

Social-Communication

NOTE

Two additional forms, the Social-Communication Observation Form (SCOF) and the Social-Communication Summary Form (SCSF; Appendix C of Volume 1) can be used to collect, record, and analyze the child's social-communication behavior. They are recommended for use in scoring the Social-Communication Area of the AEPS Child Observation Data Recording Form.

Some children have difficulty with production of the speech sounds of language (i.e., articulation disorder). The AEPS Test does not provide a formalized procedure for assessing speech skills. Consult a qualified specialist to assess the child's articulation skills. The interventionist is encouraged to share the SCOF information with the specialist, as it will provide valuable information regarding the child's speech skills within conversation.

CAUTION

Young children acquiring more than one language simultaneously initially learn vocabulary without distinguishing between languages. The number of words in a child's vocabulary, therefore, should be counted as the *total* number of words or word approximations the child is using in *both* languages. This principle holds for toddlers learning English as a second language, as well as for children from bilingual and multilingual homes. Typically developing children do not reliably and consistently sort languages into separate systems until they acquire cognitive skills of categorization and classification.

Young children from bilingual homes or who are learning English as a second language should always be assessed for comprehension in both languages and, if possible, in multiple settings. Children may use the family's native language predominantly at home and English at a center-based program, even if they have more sophisticated skills in the native language. An accurate measure of comprehension, therefore, includes presenting AEPS Test items in any language to which the child is regularly exposed.

STRAND A — Prelinguistic Communicative Interactions

GOAL 1   Turns and looks toward person speaking

CRITERION   Child turns to and looks toward the face of a speaker for at least 5 seconds. Speaker must be within 3 feet of the child.

Objective 1.1   Turns and looks toward object and person speaking

CRITERION   Child turns to and looks toward an object for at least 5 seconds while another person holds the object and comments on it. Object and speaker must be within 3 feet of child.

Objective 1.2   Turns and looks toward noise-producing object

CRITERION   Child turns to and looks toward a noise-producing object for at least 5 seconds. The object must be within 3 feet of the child.

GOAL 2   Follows person's gaze to establish joint attention

CRITERION   Child turns and looks in the direction of a person's gaze while that person looks at an object, person, and/or event. The child's glance must be longer than 1 second.

Objective 2.1   Follows person's pointing gesture to establish joint attention

CRITERION   Child looks in the direction of a person's pointing gesture while that person looks at an object, person, and/or event and comments on it. The child's glance must be longer than 1 second.

Objective 2.2   Looks toward an object

CRITERION   Child looks in the direction of an object when a person presents the object within child's reach. The child's glance must be longer than 1 second.

Social-Communication

GOAL 3   Engages in vocal exchanges by babbling

CRITERION   Child engages in two or more consecutive vocal exchanges with other people by babbling (e.g., child babbles, person imitates child, and child responds by babbling again; adult says, "Hi, baby," child responds by saying, "Ba-ba-ba"; adult repeats, "Hi, baby," and child responds, "Ba-ba-ba-ba"). An exchange includes a response from both the child and the other person.

Objective 3.1   Engages in vocal exchanges by cooing

CRITERION   Child engages in two or more consecutive vocal exchanges with other people by cooing (e.g., child coos or gurgles, person imitates child, and child responds by cooing or gurgling again; adult says, "Here's your bottle," child responds by cooing; adult asks, "Are you hungry?" and child coos again). An exchange includes a response from both the child and the other person.

Transition to Words

Note   *Refer to the SCOF and the SCSF (located in Appendix C of Volume 1) for scoring this strand.*

GOAL 1   Gains person's attention and refers to an object, person, and/or event

CRITERION   Child gains a person's attention (e.g., looks at, reaches for, touches, vocalizes) and then points to an object, person, and/or event (e.g., child looks at a person and then points to ball, child pulls on a person's arm and then points out the window).

Objective 1.1   Responds with a vocalization and gesture to simple questions

CRITERION   Child responds to simple questions with a vocalization and gesture (e.g., adult asks, "Want up?" and child reaches for adult and says, "Ba-ba-ba"; adult asks, "Where's mama?" and child points to mother and says, "Ma-ma"; adult asks, "All done?" and child shakes head and says, "Na-na").

Objective 1.2   Points to an object, person, and/or event

CRITERION   Child points to an object, person, and/or event (e.g., child points to a picture when looking at a book, child points to other children playing).

Objective 1.3   Gestures and/or vocalizes to greet others

CRITERION   Child waves arm and/or vocalizes when greeting and when leaving others (e.g., familiar person leaves room and child waves and vocalizes, "Bye-bye"; when going to bed, child vocalizes, "Na-na"; when parent enters the room, child waves arm and says, "Hi").

Objective 1.4   Uses gestures and/or vocalizations to protest actions and/or reject objects or people

CRITERION   Child responds with gestures and/or vocalizations to protest actions and/or reject objects or people (e.g., adult presents food to child; child turns from food, pushes it away, and/or makes a negative sound).

GOAL 2   Uses consistent word approximations

CRITERION   Child uses 10 consistent word approximations to refer to objects, people, and/or events (e.g., child reaches for ball and says, "Ba"; child says, "Ba-ba" and points to bottle; child looks at juice and says, "Ju").

Objective 2.1   Uses consistent consonant–vowel combinations

CRITERION   Child uses consistent speech–sound combinations to refer to objects, people, and/or events (e.g., child points to truck and says, "Da"; child reaches for ball and says, "Ga"). Sounds may be unrelated to actual label but are used to consistently refer to the same object, person, and/or event.

Objective 2.2   Uses nonspecific consonant–vowel combinations and/or jargon

CRITERION   Child babbles using speech-like sounds with rising and falling intonation; for example, child looks at parent and vocalizes a sequence of speech-like sounds (e.g., "ah-ba-ba-da").

Objective 2.3   Vocalizes to express affective states

CRITERION   Child indicates different feelings through vocalizations and intonations. The child may coo when content, whine when wanting attention, or scream when upset. The child's vocalization should clearly indicate his or her state.

Objective 2.4   Vocalizes open syllables

CRITERION   Child vocalizes sounds other than crying. The child produces at least two different vowel sounds during spontaneous vocalizations. The vowel sounds are typically prolonged in a sing-song manner (i.e., cooing).

Comprehension of Words and Sentences

GOAL 1 Locates objects, people, and/or events without contextual cues

CRITERION   Without contextual cues, the child locates (e.g., looks at, reaches for, touches, points to) at least 20 familiar objects, people, and/or events when named by another person (e.g., parent asks, "Where's Daddy?" when Daddy is in the yard and child goes to the window and points to father).

Objective 1.1 Locates common objects, people, and/or events in unfamiliar pictures

CRITERION   Child locates (e.g., looks at, reaches for, touches, points to) at least 20 common objects, people, and/or events in unfamiliar pictures when named by another person (e.g., persons says, "Show me horse," and child points to a horse in a book that is unfamiliar). The pictures should not have been used previously in the child's training.

Objective 1.2 Locates common objects, people, and/or events in familiar pictures

CRITERION   Child locates (e.g., looks at, reaches for, touches, points to) at least 10 common objects, people, and/or events in familiar pictures when named by another person (e.g., child points to a ball, dog, or truck in a familiar picture book).

Objective 1.3 Locates common objects, people, and/or events with contextual cues

CRITERION   With contextual cues, the child locates (e.g., looks at, reaches for, touches, points to) at least five common objects, people, and/or events when named by another person (e.g., when playing with dishes, a person asks the child to "show me the cup," and child picks the cup; when asked, "Where's Daddy?" child looks toward his or her father).

Objective 1.4 Recognizes own name

CRITERION   Child responds differently to his or her name than to general verbalizations (e.g., child may brighten, increase his or her activity level, smile, turn toward a person, vocalize when his or her name is called).

Objective 1.5   **Quiets to familiar voice**

CRITERION   Child quiets in response to caregiver or other familiar voice (e.g., when the child is fussing, he or she quiets; his or her activity level decreases when spoken to with comforting tones by a familiar adult).

GOAL 2   **Carries out two-step direction without contextual cues**

CRITERION   Child responds with appropriate motor action to a two-step direction that does not relate to the immediate context (e.g., when a doll is not present in the immediate environment, another person tells the child, "Go get your doll and put it on the table," and child gets doll and puts it on the table).

Objective 2.1   **Carries out two-step direction with contextual cues**

CRITERION   Child responds with appropriate motor action to a two-step direction that relates to the immediate context (e.g., when playing with dolls and dishes, another person asks child, "get the cup and give baby a drink," and child gets the cup and pretends to give the doll a drink).

Objective 2.2   **Carries out one-step direction without contextual cues**

CRITERION   Child responds with appropriate motor action to a one-step direction that does not relate to the immediate context (e.g., another person tells the child, "Get the ball" when it is not immediately present, and child gets the ball).

Objective 2.3   **Carries out one-step direction with contextual cues**

CRITERION   Child responds with appropriate motor action to a one-step direction that relates to the immediate context (e.g., person tells the child, "Get your coat" when standing in front of the coat rack, and child gets the coat).

STRAND D

Production of Social-Communicative Signals, Words, and Sentences

Note   *Refer to the SCOF and the SCSF (located in Appendix C of Volume 1) for scoring this strand.*

GOAL 1   Uses 50 single words

CRITERION   Child uses 50 single words appropriately, which includes at least five descriptive words, five action words, two pronouns, 15 labeling words, and three proper names. (See Objectives 1.1–1.5 for specific directions.)

Note   *Child must score a 2 on Objectives 1.1–1.5 in order to score a 2 on Goal 1. If the child scores a 1 and/or a 0 on some of these objectives, then score Goal 1 with a 1. If the child scores a 0 on all of these objectives, then score Goal 1 as a 0.*

Objective 1.1   Uses five descriptive words

CRITERION   Child uses five different descriptive words (e.g., big, little, hot, red, blue) appropriately (e.g., child touches a cup of tea and says, "hot," child shows muddy hands and says, "dirty").

Objective 1.2   Uses five action words

CRITERION   Child uses five different action words (e.g., open, go, eat, sit, run) appropriately (e.g., child gives box of animal crackers to adult and says, "open," child kicks ball and says, "kick").

Objective 1.3   Uses two pronouns

CRITERION   Child uses two different pronouns (e.g., me, mine, it, my, you, this) appropriately (e.g., child looks at photograph and says, "me"; child holds a toy and says, "mine").

Objective 1.4   Uses 15 object and/or event labels

CRITERION   Child uses 15 different object and/or event labels (e.g., ball, cup, hat, bubbles) appropriately (e.g., child sees cat and says, "kitty"; child says, "bubbles" when watching adult blow bubbles).

Social-Communication

Objective 1.5   Uses three proper names

CRITERION   Child uses three different proper names (e.g., Mama, James, Daddy, Spot) appropriately (e.g., child looks at parent and says, "Mama"; when playing with a friend, child calls out, "James").

GOAL 2   Uses two-word utterances

CRITERION   Child uses a variety of two-word utterances to express:

- Agent–action, action–object, and agent–object
- Possession
- Location
- Description
- Recurrence
- Negation

(See Objectives 2.1–2.6 for specific directions.)

Note   *Child must score a 2 on Objectives 2.1–2.6 in order to score a 2 on Goal 2. If the child scores a 1 and/or a 0 on some of these objectives, then score Goal 2 with a 1. If the child scores a 0 on all of these objectives, then score Goal 2 with a 0.*

Objective 2.1   Uses two-word utterances to express agent–action, action–object, and agent–object

CRITERION   Child uses 10 different two-word utterances to express agent–action (Mama go), action–object (roll ball), and agent–object (Daddy truck) (e.g., child watches father eating and says, "Daddy eat" [agent–action]; child points to baby and says, "He cry" [agent–action]; child watches another child pushing a toy truck and says, "Push truck" [action–object]; child holds up cookies and says, "Eat cookie" [action–object]; child watches mother putting on a hat and says, "Mommy hat" [agent–object]; child points to toy and says, "My truck" [agent–object]).

Objective 2.2   Uses two-word utterances to express possession

CRITERION   Child uses five different two-word utterances to express possession (e.g., child takes book from peer and says, "My book"; child sees mother's car and says, "Mommy's car").

Objective 2.3   Uses two-word utterances to express location

CRITERION   Child uses five different two-word utterances to indicate location (e.g., child points to parent and says,
"There Mommy"; child reaches toward another person, then looks at wagon and says, "In wagon").

Objective 2.4   Uses two-word utterances to describe objects, people, and/or events

CRITERION   Child uses five different two-word utterances to describe objects, people, and/or events (e.g., child
watches parent cooking, points to pan and says,
"Pan hot"; child points to tractor and says, "Big
tractor"; child says, "Red block," when playing with
blocks).

Objective 2.5   Uses two-word utterances to express recurrence

CRITERION   Child uses five different two-word utterances to indicate recurrence (e.g., child holds up cup and says,
"More juice"; when being pulled in wagon, child
says, "Go again").

Objective 2.6   Uses two-word utterances to express negation

CRITERION   Child uses five different two-word utterances to express rejection, disappearance, and/or denial (e.g.,
child gives wind-up toy to parent and says, "Not
go"; child finishes a cup of juice and says, "No
more").

GOAL 3   Uses three-word utterances

CRITERION   Child uses a variety of three-word utterances to
express:

- Negation

- Questions

- Action–object–location

- Agent–action–object

(See Objectives 3.1–3.4 for specific directions.)

Note   *Child must score a 2 on Objectives 3.1–3.4 in order
to score a 2 on Goal 3. If the child scores a 1 and/or
a 0 on some of the objectives, then score Goal 3
with a 1. If the child scores all of these objectives
with a 0, then score Goal 3 with a 0.*

Objective 3.1 Uses three-word negative utterances

CRITERION   Child uses five different three-word utterances that include a negative term (e.g., no, not, don't, can't, won't; child says, "No baby's coat"; child says, "No do that").

Objective 3.2 Asks questions

CRITERION   Child asks five different two- and three-word questions using "Wh-" words (e.g., what, where) or using raising intonation (e.g., child goes to coat rack and asks, "Where my coat?"; child watches parent prepare food and asks with raising intonation, "We eat lunch?"; child watches friend playing and says, "What doing?").

Objective 3.3 Uses three-word action–object–location utterances

CRITERION   Child uses five different three-word utterances to express action–object–location (e.g., child says, "Put baby in"; "Roll ball here").

Objective 3.4 Uses three-word agent–action–object utterances

CRITERION   Child uses five different three-word utterances to express agent–action–object (e.g., child says, "I blow bubble"; "He throw ball"; "Baby drink milk"; "James drive car").

AEPS™

Social Area
Birth to Three Years

LIST OF AEPS TEST ITEMS

Social

109

CAUTION

The development of social skills is closely related to and interdependent on the development of cognitive, communication, and adaptive skills. Therefore, data from all areas should be considered by the examiner when reviewing Social Area items. The influence of cultural values on children's social behavior should also be considered during administration of the Social Area.

Interaction with Familiar Adults

GOAL 1 Responds appropriately to familiar adult's affect

CRITERION   Child appropriately responds to familiar adult's affect, including facial expressions, gestures, tone,
requests, comments, or corrections (e.g., when familiar adult enters the room, child smiles in recognition; when familiar adult asks child for a hug,
child gives adult hug; when familiar adult corrects
child's behavior, child looks sad or cries; when familiar adult affectionately pats child on the back,
child pats adult on the arm).

Objective 1.1 Displays affection toward familiar adult

CRITERION   Child spontaneously hugs, kisses, pats, touches, and/
or reaches toward a familiar adult (e.g., upon adult's
return, child hugs adult; during positive interactions
or simple games, child reaches for and touches or
pats adult affectionately).

Objective 1.2 Responds appropriately to familiar adult's affective tone

CRITERION   Child responds with socially appropriate affect to familiar adult's affective tone (e.g., child laughs, smiles,
or produces part of interactive game in response to
adult's positive tone; child cries, frowns, turns away
in response to adult's displeasure or corrections).

Objective 1.3 Smiles in response to familiar adult

CRITERION   Child smiles in response to an approach, vocalization, smile, and/or appearance of a familiar adult
(e.g., as adult comments on child's play, child smiles
at adult then continues playing; as child plays on
floor with preferred toy, adult sits down to join,
child looks up and smiles).

GOAL 2 Initiates and maintains interaction with familiar adult

CRITERION   Child initiates and maintains interaction with familiar adult for two or more consecutive exchanges. An
exchange consists of a response from the child and
from the adult (e.g., child gains adult attention then
puts cloth over own head, adult says, "Peekaboo,"

and child removes cloth, adult smiles, child laughs; child claps hands, adult says, "Pat-a-cake," child claps hands again, and adult says, "Pat-a-cake").

Objective 2.1   Initiates simple social game with familiar adult

CRITERION   Child initiates simple social game with familiar adult (e.g., child claps hands and adult says, "Pat-a-cake"; child crawls under table then peeks out at adult and adult says, "Boo"; child rolls a ball toward adult and adult rolls it back).

Note   *Objects that can be used in interactive games (e.g., ball for rolling, blanket for Peekaboo) may be useful.*

Objective 2.2   Responds to familiar adult's social behavior

CRITERION   Child responds to familiar adult's social behavior (e.g., child waves "bye-bye" in response to adult's good-bye; adult peeks at child around a corner, then retreats, and child peeks at adult and laughs).

Objective 2.3   Uses familiar adults for comfort, closeness, or physical contact

CRITERION   Child seeks comfort, closeness, or physical contact from familiar adult by directing position, proximity, gestures, expressions, gaze, or vocalizations toward him or her across a variety of situations (i.e., when hurt, sad, needs comfort, needs reassurance; e.g., child climbs into parent's lap and hugs him or her after being examined by a doctor; child stands next to caregiver and clings to his or her leg as a big dog approaches; child extends hand to parent and asks him or her to kiss it better; when favorite peer has to go home, child expresses sadness by leaning on caregiver for several minutes).

GOAL 3   Initiates and maintains communicative exchange with familiar adult

CRITERION   Child initiates and maintains a communicative exchange by directing gestures, signs, vocalizations, and/or verbalizations toward adult for two or more consecutive exchanges (e.g., child holds up keys and says, "Ke-ke," adult says, "Yes, those are keys," child says, "Ke," adult asks, "Where does the key go?" and child gestures toward the door; child points to cup that is out of reach and vocalizes to adult, adult says, "Cup," child reaches for cup and looks at

adult, adult asks, "Oh, you want a drink?" and child
nods). An exchange consists of a response from the
child and from the adult.

Objective 3.1   Initiates communication with familiar adult

CRITERION   Child initiates communication by directing gestures, signs, vocalizations, and/or verbalizations toward familiar adult (e.g., child holds up a toy car and
says "Ka"; child tugs at adult's leg to gain adult's attention then points to juice; child raises arms toward adult and vocalizes; child points to picture in
book then looks at adult).

Objective 3.2   Responds to communication from familiar adult

CRITERION   Child responds to familiar adult's communication
by gesturing, signing, verbalizing, following requests,
and/or attending (e.g., adult says, "Wave bye-bye,"
child waves hand; adult asks, "Where is the ball?"
and child points to picture of ball; adult says child's
name and child turns toward adult).

STRAND B
Interaction with Environment

GOAL 1 Meets observable physical needs in socially appropriate ways

CRITERION Child uses socially appropriate ways to meet observable physical needs (e.g., child washes hands or requests help from adult when hands are dirty; child attempts to remove wet or soiled clothing; child requests adult help when injuries occur; child gets a tissue and blows own nose; child goes to adult and tugs at soiled diaper). Observable physical needs can include dirty hands or clothing, injury, runny nose, or soiled diapers, but *do not* include more internal physical needs such as hunger, thirst, or rest.

Objective 1.1 Meets internal physical needs of hunger, thirst, and rest

CRITERION Child meets internal physical needs of hunger, thirst, and rest (e.g., child goes to the cupboard and gets a cracker or to the refrigerator to get juice; child indicates thirst to adult by holding up cup; after rough-and-tumble play, child rests or naps).

Objective 1.2 Uses appropriate strategies to self-soothe

CRITERION Child is able to self-regulate by maintaining or regaining composure from high emotional responses including crying, anger, fear, or frustration to more relaxed or low emotional self-expressions (e.g., child who bursts into tears after being licked by a dog recovers and calmly watches the dog play with a ball; child who shows great fear at the dentist is able to get in the chair and take a treat from the dentist; child who cries when mom's keys are taken away, recovers and finds another toy to play with; child who becomes frustrated and whines when leg gets stuck on the riding toy, moves on and runs with peers after getting help off the toy; child uses familiar objects like pacifier, blanket, thumb, or self-talking, and/or closeness with adult to calm self in stressful situations).

GOAL 2   Participates in established social routines

CRITERION   When given general verbal and/or contextual cues, child performs a series of responses associated with established social routines such as mealtime, toileting, dressing/ undressing, bathing/washing, naptime/ bedtime, and/or classroom events (e.g., as adult begins to set table and/or says, "It's lunch time," child washes hands, gets bib, and goes to the table; when adult turns on bath water, child goes to the tub, takes off clothes, and gets tub toys).

Note   *Familiar objects or environmental prompts associated with routine events may be necessary; for example:*

- *Dinner: silverware or food taken out of the refrigerator*

- *Toileting: potty chair*

- *Bathing: change of clothes or tub of water toys*

- *Nap: blanket and pillow or cots from the closet*

Objective 2.1   Responds to established social routines

CRITERION   When given general verbal and/or contextual cues, the child performs a single response associated with established social routines such as mealtime, toileting, dressing/undressing, bathing/washing, naptime/ bedtime, and/or classroom events (e.g., as adult begins to set table and/or says, "It's lunch time," child sits down at the table; when adult says, "It's time to take a nap," child goes and gets blanket; when adult says "bath time," child goes to tub and removes clothes).

Interaction with Peers

GOAL 1   Initiates and maintains interaction with peer

CRITERION   Child initiates and maintains interaction with peer for two or more consecutive exchanges (e.g., child hides in cupboard, peer knocks on door, child opens door and laughs, and peer closes door and knocks again; child uses bricks to build wall, peer adds additional bricks, and the two children look at each other, laugh, knock the wall down and begin building again; child approaches peer, reaches for peer's toy and offers own toy, peer turns away, child taps peer on shoulder and offers toy again). An exchange consists of a response from the child and from the peer.

Note   *Toys that encourage interaction should be available (e.g., balls, blocks, beanbags, puppets, dishes, boxes).*

Objective 1.1   Initiates social behavior toward peer

CRITERION   Child initiates social behavior toward peer (e.g., child gives toy to peer; child smiles at peer; child directs communication toward peer; child waves at peer; child calls out peer's name).

Objective 1.2   Responds appropriately to peer's social behavior

CRITERION   Child responds with socially appropriate affect to peer's social behavior (e.g., peer says, "Hi," child says, "Hi"; when peer hits child, child says, "Don't"; peer offers cracker, child takes it).

Objective 1.3   Plays near one or two peers

CRITERION   Child maintains play near one or two peers (e.g., child plays with toy cars and a ramp while nearby in the same room his peer plays with Legos; two children play in the dramatic play area, one plays with dolls and the other pretends to cook; two children work side by side, each putting pieces into their own puzzle). Children do not need to be playing in the same activity or using the same toys.

Objective 1.4   Observes peers

CRITERION   Child watches peers who are playing nearby.

Objective 1.5   Entertains self by playing appropriately with toys

CRITERION   Child plays appropriately with toys without adult assistance (e.g., with or without adult in the room, child plays with toys by him- or herself; in a small classroom with other children, child selects toys and plays by him- or herself). Child may or may not be close to adult or peers.

Note   *A young child who enjoys repetitious play is allowed to pass over this item even if he or she tends to play with a limited number of toys in a repetitious manner.*

GOAL 2   Initiates and maintains communicative exchange with peer

CRITERION   Child initiates and maintains a communicative exchange by directing gestures, signs, vocalizations, and/or verbalizations toward peer for two or more consecutive exchanges (e.g., child says, "Let's play cars," peer says, "Okay," child rolls car and says, "Zoom," and peer says, "Zoom zoom"; when eating snack with a peer, child asks peer "That your cookie?" Peer clutches cookie and nods head, child asks, "Can I have one?" and peer says, "No"). An exchange consists of a response from the child and from the peer.

Note   • *Toys that encourage interactions, such as balls, blocks, cars, dress-up clothes, puppets, musical toys, and toy buildings, should be available for use.*

• *Communicative interaction may be encouraged by grouping children together with consideration for individual child interests, peer preference, and developmental levels of functioning.*

Objective 2.1   Initiates communication with peer

CRITERION   Child initiates communication by directing gestures, signs, vocalizations, and/or verbalizations toward peer (e.g., child points and says to peer, "See that"; child pats his or her pocket and says to peer, "I have money").

Objective 2.2   Responds to communication from peer

CRITERION   Child responds to communication from peer by gesturing, signing, vocalizing, and/or verbalizing (e.g., child approaches peer who calls his or her name, peer waves and says "Hello," child smiles and waves back; two children pretend to camp, peer says, "bedtime," and child closes the tent flap and puts a blanket over them).

Social

SECTION

III

AEPS Test: Three to Six Years

OVERVIEW OF THE AEPS TEST: THREE TO SIX YEARS

The AEPS Test: Three to Six Years covers the developmental period from 3 to 6 years and is generally appropriate for children whose chronological age is from 3 to 9 years. The AEPS Test is composed of six areas; each area encompasses a particular set of skills, behaviors, or information that is traditionally seen as developmentally related.

- **Fine Motor Area:** Items in this area assess specific arm and hand movements in activities such as manipulating objects with two hands, scissors skills, and writing.

- **Gross Motor Area:** Items in this area assess ability to use gross motor skills for mobility in play activities.

- **Adaptive Area:** Items in this area assess mealtime skills such as drinking from a cup and eating with a fork and spoon. This area also measures skills used to maintain personal hygiene and dressing.

- **Cognitive Area:** Items in this area assess use of various concepts, problem-solving skills, recall, grouping and sequencing objects and events, premath, early literacy skills, and play skills.

- **Social-Communication Area:** Items in this area assess receptive, expressive, and social skills of communication.

- **Social Area:** Items in this area assess interactions with peers, responses to the environment, knowledge of self and others, and group participation skills.

TEST ORGANIZATION AND SCORING

Before using the AEPS Test, the user should carefully read and review the material contained in Chapter 3 of Volume 1. Chapter 3 provides detailed information on the content and organization of the AEPS Test. In addition, scoring criteria, notes, and options are discussed in Chapter 3. Consequently, these topics are reviewed only briefly in the current section.

Organizational Structure

The AEPS Test: Three to Six Years addresses six developmental areas: Fine Motor, Gross Motor, Adaptive, Cognitive, Social-Communication, and Social. Each area is divided into strands, which in turn contain associated goals/objectives. Each strand and goal/objective have an index letter or number for easy referral. Strands are identified with capital letters (e.g., Strand A, Strand B, Strand C). Goals are identified with whole numbers (e.g., 1, 2, 3) and are listed under their respective strands. Objectives are listed under their respective goals and are identified with a decimal number (e.g., 1.1, 1.2, 1.3) that reflects the goal number; for example, objectives associated with Goal 3 are indexed as 3.1, 3.2, and 3.3.

Item Criterion and Scoring

Each AEPS Test item is accompanied by a performance criterion. The test user should use the criterion as the standard for scoring the child's response. A three-point scoring option should be employed consistently across items. To determine whether a child's response should be scored 2, 1, or 0, specific criteria are provided for each AEPS Test item (i.e., for each goal/objective). It is essential to compare children's performance with each item's criterion before recording a score. Criteria are found under the description of each test item. Table 5 presents a summary of scoring guidelines when information is collected through direct test procedures and observation.

It should be emphasized that arranging antecedent conditions to help elicit responses from children does not necessarily constitute direct testing; for example, placing silverware within a child's reach to assess eating skills is not direct testing. Having available and accessible objects of different colors, sizes, and configurations to assess a child's early concept understanding would not be considered direct testing. Rather, *direct testing* refers to conducting specific trial-by-trial procedures generally apart from routine or play activities in which specific and direct antecedents are given; for example, the child is repeatedly shown a set of pictures and asked to name them.

In addition to the three-option scoring codes, notes are provided to allow users to record other important information about a child's performance on AEPS Test items; for example, a child may use adaptive equipment such as a communication board to perform an item of labeling objects and events. Because the child can demonstrate the concept of labeling independently and consistently, the item is scored 2, but it is also scored with a note (i.e., M = modification/adaptation in this case). Notes alert teams to important information that should be considered when interpreting AEPS Test information, designing subsequent intervention plans, and conducting future evaluations. Modifications of items for children with disabilities is encouraged; however, when such modifications occur, they should be noted. A description of the six notes and associated scoring guidelines is contained in Table 6.

Table 5.   Scoring guidelines for observation and direct test procedures

Score	Description of performance
Observation	
2 = Consistently meets criterion	Child consistently performs the item as specified in the criterion.
	Child performs the item independently.
	Behavior is a functional part of the child's repertoire.
	Child uses the skill across time, materials, settings, and people.
1 = Inconsistently meets criterion	Child does not consistently perform the item as specified in the criterion.
	Child performs the item with assistance.
	Child does not perform all components of the item or does not meet all aspects of the specified criterion (i.e., the behavior is emerging).
	Child performs the item only under specific situations or conditions (i.e., with certain people or in certain settings).
0 = Does not meet criterion	Child does not yet perform the item as specified in the criterion when given repeated opportunities or assistance or when modifications and adaptations are made.
	Child was not observed performing the item because it is not expected based on knowledge of development (e.g., the child's chronological age is 6 months and he or she would not be expected to perform such items as categorizing similar objects, copying simple shapes, or walking up and down stairs).
Direct test	
2 = Consistently meets criterion	Child performs the item as specified in the criterion on at least two out of three trials.
	Child performs the item independently on two out of three trials.
	Child uses the skill on two out of three trials across time, materials, settings, and people.
1 = Inconsistently meets criterion	Child performs the item as specified in the criterion on one out of three trials.
	Child performs the item with assistance on one out of three trials.
	Child performs only portions of the item or certain aspects of the specified criterion on one out of three trials.
	Child performs the item under one situation or one set of conditions.
0 = Does not meet criterion	Child does not yet perform the item as specified in the criterion on zero out of three trials when assistance is provided or when modifications and adaptations are made.
	Child was not observed performing the item because it is not expected based on knowledge of development (e.g., the child's chronological age is 6 months and he or she would not be expected to perform such items as categorizing similar objects, copying (simple shapes, or walking up and down stairs), thus no trials are given.

Table 6. Notes, definitions, and scoring guidelines

Note	Definitions and scoring guidelines
A	**Assistance provided**

A **Assistance provided**

When a child is provided with some form of *assistance,* an A should be noted in the space next to the performance score box. If assistance is provided, then the only scores allowed are 1 and 0 because a score of 2 indicates full independent performance. Assistance includes any direct verbal or physical prompt, cue, or model that assists the child in initiating or performing the desired behavior. A general direction given to the child to initiate the behavior is not considered assistance. For example, the directive, "Put on your coat" is not considered assistance, but physically holding out the coat and helping the child insert his or her arms is assistance for the AEPS Test item Puts on Front-Opening Garment.

B **Behavior interfered**

At times, a child's behavior may interfere with the demonstration of the desired skill. In such cases, the item may be scored 1 or 0 with a B noted next to the performance score. This note indicates that the child may have the skill, but disruptive or noncompliant behavior interfered with its demonstration.

D **Direct test**

When the examiner directly elicits a behavior, a D is noted next to the performance score and the guidelines for determining the score presented in Table 5 should be followed.

M **Modification/adaptation**

At times, an examiner may need to modify the stated *criteria* (e.g., rate or mode of response) or adapt the *environment/materials* (e.g., adaptive equipment is necessary) to assess children with sensory or motor disabilities. When *modifications* are made in gathering child performance information, an M is noted next to the performance score and a 2, 1, or 0 is used.

Q **Quality of performance**

At times, a child is able to perform a skill independently, but the team feels the quality of the performance hinders the ability to meet criteria. At other times, a child is able to meet or partially meet the stated criteria, but the team wishes to continue strengthening the quality of performance. When the quality of the performance is in question, teams are encouraged to use a Q in the notes accompanied by a score of 2 or 1.

R **Report**

When an item is assessed by *report,* an R is noted next to the performance score. Report is used under one of three conditions:

- When assessment information is collected by another person or documented source (e.g., written evaluation), the item is scored 2, 1, or 0, and an R is noted.
- When the item is judged inappropriate because it assesses a primitive or developmentally easier response (e.g., sucking on a nipple when the child is able to drink from a cup), the item is scored 2 and an R is noted.
- When the item is judged inappropriate because it is too advanced or beyond the child's developmental level (e.g., walking when the child is unable to stand), the item is scored 0 and an R is noted.

Test Materials

No standard or required set of materials or objects is necessary for the administration of the AEPS Test items. Commonly available toys and objects can be used in the administration of all items. Toys and other objects that are of interest to the child are likely to produce more accurate assessment information than using materials that are of limited interest to the child. Therefore, before administering test items, it is essential to talk with caregivers to determine what type of materials the child prefers. It is also important to select age-appropriate materials. Suggested materials for each developmental area are listed below.

Materials for AEPS Test: Three to Six Years

Fine Motor

To assess manipulation of objects/materials with two hands
    Beads and string, Tinkertoys, small Legos, markers/pens with caps, buttons on garments, pop beads, jars with lids, soap and washcloth
To assess cutting
    Child-size scissors, spring-loaded scissors, or other adapted scissors
    Paper, string, playdough
To assess writing
    Chalkboard
    Paints
    Chalk, pencil, crayon, marker, paintbrush
    Simple and complex shapes drawn on cards or paper
    Paper on which child's own first name is printed

Gross Motor

To assess climbing
    Stairs
To assess jumping
    Long, thin object (e.g., rope, tape, chalk line, stick)
    Low platform (e.g., curb, step, raised platform) at least 10 inches high
To assess ball skills
    Balls 8 inches in diameter, 6 inches in diameter and hand-size
To assess riding skills
    Two-wheel bicycle with and without training wheels

Adaptive

To assess mealtime skills
  Semi-solid foods such as applesauce and yogurt
  Chewy foods such as meats and dried fruits
  Hard foods such as apples, raw vegetables, and pretzels
  Soft foods such as bananas, cooked vegetables, and macaroni
  Foods to spear such as meat, vegetables, and pieces of fruit
  Foods to scoop such as soup, cereal, and applesauce
  Foods with inedible parts removed prior to eating such as banana, hard-
      boiled egg, candy in wrapper, crackers in box
  Foods that can be spread with knife such as peanut butter, cream cheese,
      and jam
  Utensils such as fork, blunt-edged knife, and spoon
  Dish
  Cup or glass
  Liquids such as milk, juice, and water
  Containers for pouring, such as pitcher and bottle, and for filling, such as
      cup, bowl, and glass
To assess personal hygiene
  Toilet or potty chair
  Tissue
  Toothbrush, toothpaste
  Soap, water, towel, tub, or shower
  Sink or wash basin
  Brush, comb
To assess dressing
  Shoes with shoelaces
  Shirt, pants, dress that fastens with buttons/snaps/Velcro fasteners
  Hood with string
  Coat, jacket, sweater that fastens with zipper
  Front-opening garment (e.g., blouse, shirt, coat
  Pullover garment (e.g., T-shirt, dress, sweater)
  Shoes, sandals, slippers
  Underpants, shorts, skirt

Cognitive

To assess concepts
  Objects of various colors, shapes, and sizes
  Objects that can be identified by qualitative features
To assess categorizing
  Three sets of objects that can be grouped in different ways (e.g., category,
      function, attribute)
  Two sets of objects that can be grouped according to function (e.g., things
      to eat, things to wear, things to ride on)
  Sets of objects that can be arranged in a series according to length or size

To assess sequencing
   At least three sequential pictures that depict a story or event
To assess imaginary play
   Dolls/stuffed animals, baby carriage, doll house, doll bed
   Dress-up clothes
To assess following rules
   Toys and/or objects used in games with rules
To assess premath
   A set of 20 objects
   Cards, books, or other materials with printed numerals from 1 to 10
   Cards or other materials with printed numerals from 1 to 10 and printed
     letters
To assess phonological awareness and emergent reading
   Writing tools, paper and books
   Cards with printed letters and common words (e.g., stop, dog, cat, cup)
   Card with child's first name

Social-Communication

Various materials of interest to the child to encourage communication

Social

Various materials of interest to the child to encourage interaction with adults and
   peers and participation in group activities

AEPS™

Fine Motor Area
Three to Six Years

LIST OF AEPS TEST ITEMS

NOTE

Using two hands together in a coordinated manner is often called *bilateral motor coordination* and follows a developmental progression from simple to more complex. When first learning to perform a two-handed task, the child will use one hand to hold or steady an object and the other to manipulate; for example, holding down paper while coloring, holding a nail while hammering, or holding a cup while pouring juice. Eventually, bilateral motor coordination involves the two hands performing different movements. Examples of these bilateral motor skills include buttoning clothes by using one hand to keep the button hole open and the other hand to manipulate the button through the hole, using hands to tie shoelaces, or cutting out shapes with scissors.

CAUTION

Children with cerebral palsy or other motor disorders may exhibit unusual or atypical patterns of movement; for example, the child may move arms or legs stiffly or in an uncoordinated manner, or one arm and/or leg may not be used as well as the other. Referral and consultation with specialists (e.g., occupational therapist, physical therapist) is critical. Scores on the AEPS Test items should reflect poor quality of movement by scoring items using either a 1 or 0. In addition, a scoring note of Q for Quality of performance should be used to provide the most accurate information about the child's performance. If a child performs skills significantly better with one hand than the other, then scoring each hand individually may be appropriate.

Bilateral Motor Coordination

GOAL 1 Uses two hands to manipulate objects, each hand performing different movements

CRITERION   Child uses both hands to manipulate a variety of objects/toys/materials that require use of both hands at the same time but while performing different movements (e.g., child strings small beads; threads zipper and zips coat; buttons small buttons; ties shoes).

Objective 1.1 Holds object with one hand while the other hand manipulates

CRITERION   Child performs any two-handed task using one hand to hold or steady an object while other hand manipulates the object or performs a movement (e.g., holds paper while drawing; holds glass while pouring liquid from pitcher; steadies container while removing playdough; holds book while turning the pages).

GOAL 2 Cuts out shapes with curved lines

CRITERION   Child uses scissors to cut out shapes with curved lines (e.g., circles, ovals, magazine pictures). Child uses paper with printed shapes or pictures (at least 3 inches in diameter) and cuts close to line, shape, or picture. Child holds scissors between thumb and first two fingers of one hand and holds paper with other hand.

Objective 2.1 Cuts out shapes with straight lines

CRITERION   Child uses scissors to cut out simple shapes with straight lines (e.g., squares, rectangles, triangles). Child uses paper with printed shapes or pictures (at least 3 inches in diameter) and cuts close to shape or picture. Child holds scissors between thumb and first two fingers of one hand and holds paper with other hand.

Objective 2.2 Cuts paper in two

CRITERION   Child uses scissors to cut paper in two. Child needs to make at least three consecutive cuts. Edge may be jagged. Child holds scissors between thumb and first two fingers of one hand and holds paper with other hand.

Emergent Writing

GOAL 1   Writes using three-finger grasp

CRITERION   Child draws or writes with crayon, marker, pencil, or other writing implement using three-finger grasp–fingers near point of implement, moving the implement primarily with finger movements rather than whole arm movements. Child is able to position writing implement with one hand by moving fingers of the writing hand rather than using two hands.

Objective 1.1   Uses three-finger grasp to hold writing implement

CRITERION   Child holds crayon, marker, pencil, or other writing implement using the thumb and first two fingers. Child may move whole arm across writing surface to write or draw.

GOAL 2   Prints pseudo-letters

CRITERION   Child uses writing instrument (e.g., crayon, marker, pencil, paintbrush) to print shapes that resemble letters and words, starting at the top of the page and moving downward from left to right on each line. The shapes produced do not need to be actual letters or words but may be invented spellings and/or pseudo-letters. (A child who is learning a language other than English may follow different conventions for that language.)

Objective 2.1   Draws using representational figures

CRITERION   Child uses writing implements to draw pictures that represent people, places, events, and objects. The drawing is either recognizable to others or the child is able to describe or label features of the drawings.

Objective 2.2   Copies complex shapes

CRITERION   Child copies shapes with angles (e.g., rectangle, square, triangle) from a drawn model (e.g., drawn on cards, paper, the sidewalk).

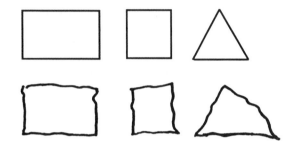

Objective 2.3   Copies simple shapes

CRITERION   Child copies shapes with circular contours or lines (e.g., circle, cross, T) from a drawn model (e.g., drawn on cards or paper)

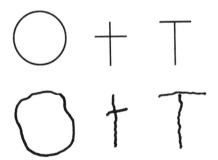

GOAL 3   Prints first name

CRITERION   Child prints own first name without model. Letters must be in correct order, but errors are permissible (e.g., letter printed backward). Name should be recognizable.

Objective 3.1   Prints three letters

CRITERION   Child prints any three upper- or lowercase letters without model. Errors are permissible (e.g., letter printed backward); however, individual letters should be recognizable. Verbal cues may be provided (e.g., "Can you write some letters?"; "Make an E").

Objective 3.2   Copies first name

CRITERION   Child copies own first name from model (e.g., paper on which child's own first name is printed). Letters should be in correct order and recognizable. Errors are permissible (e.g., letter printed backward).

Objective 3.3   Copies three letters

CRITERION   Child copies three upper- or lowercase letters from model (e.g., single letters printed on paper or cards). Printing errors are permissible (e.g., letter printed backward); however, individual letters should be recognizable.

AEPS™

Gross Motor Area
Three to Six Years

LIST OF AEPS TEST ITEMS

133

NOTE

The development of gross motor skills is viewed as the continuous acquisition of behaviors culminating in the child's ability to maintain stability in various positions (balance) and move from one position to another (positional change). Many of the skills developed in the first 3 years of life are refined during the 3–6 age range as the child achieves greater coordination and skill moving large muscles of the body; for example, a child between 2 and 3 years of age learns to jump using both feet. During the 3–6 year age range, jumping skills become more skillful allowing the child to jump forward and down from a raised surface with secure balance and use of arms and legs to assist projecting the body into space.

CAUTION

Children with cerebral palsy or other motor disorders may exhibit unusual or atypical patterns of movement; for example, the child may move arms or legs stiffly or in an uncoordinated manner, or one arm and/or leg may not be used as well as the other. Commonly observed atypical patterns of movement in children with cerebral palsy may include

- Sitting with rounded back and head resting on shoulders

- Walking on toes with legs together

Referral and consultation with specialists (e.g., occupational therapist, physical therapist) is critical. Scores on the AEPS Test items should reflect the quality of movement by scoring items with either a 1 or 0. In addition, a qualifying note of Q for Quality of performance should be used to provide the most accurate information about the child's skill level.

Gross Motor

Balance and Mobility

GOAL 1   Runs avoiding obstacles

CRITERION   Child avoids obstacles while running by controlling starts, stops, and sudden changes in direction.

Objective 1.1   Runs

CRITERION   Child runs. Trunk is inclined slightly forward, arms swing freely, legs alternately flex and extend, and there is a period of no support by either leg.

GOAL 2   Alternates feet walking up and down stairs

CRITERION   Child walks up and down stairs, alternating feet without holding handrail or wall.

Objective 2.1   Walks up and down stairs

CRITERION   Child walks up and down stairs without alternating feet. Child may hold handrail or wall with one hand for support.

STRAND B

Play Skills

GOAL 1   Jumps forward

CRITERION   Child jumps forward with feet together; hips, knees, and ankles are flexed; and body is crouched on take-off and landing. Arms lead with a vigorous forward and upward thrust, and body is fully extended as it becomes airborne. Child lands on two feet without falling. Adult may model the action (e.g., adult jumps over a rope, tape, chalk line, or stick and encourages child to jump).

Objective 1.1   Jumps in place

CRITERION   Child jumps up and down in place with hips, knees, and ankles flexed on takeoff and landing. Arms lead with a vigorous forward and upward thrust, and body extends as it becomes airborne. Child lands on two feet without falling. Adult may model action.

Objective 1.2   Jumps from platform

CRITERION   Child jumps from a low platform (e.g., curb, step, raised platform) of at least 10 inches to the supporting surface. Child lands on two feet without falling. Adult may model action.

Objective 1.3   Balances on one foot

CRITERION   Child balances on one foot for at least 3 seconds. Adult may model action.

GOAL 2   Bounces, catches, kicks, and throws ball

CRITERION   Child performs the following ball activities:

- Bounces

- Catches

- Kicks

- Throws

NOTE   *If a child's performance on all objectives was scored with a 2, then the goal is scored 2. If a child's performance on the objectives was scored with any com-*

bination of a 0, 1, or 2, then the goal is scored 1. If a child's performance on all objectives was scored with a 0, then the goal is scored 0.

Objective 2.1   Bounces ball

CRITERION   Child bounces a large ball (at least 8 inches in diameter) at least twice, using the palm of one hand.

Objective 2.2   Catches ball

CRITERION   Child catches ball at least 6 inches in diameter using palms of two hands. Ball is thrown underhand to child from a distance of 6–10 feet.

Objective 2.3   Kicks ball

CRITERION   Child kicks stationary large ball (at least 8 inches in diameter) with one foot while maintaining balance. Ideally, support leg is flexed while kicking leg swings backward and forward and follows through in direction of kick.

Objective 2.4   Throws ball

CRITERION   Child throws hand-size ball forward with one hand, using overhand throw. Throwing arm is moved backward in preparation, and child uses shoulder and elbow to throw.

GOAL 3   Skips

CRITERION   Child skips at least 15 feet, using alternating step–hop pattern.

Objective 3.1   Hops

CRITERION   Child hops forward with five or more consecutive hops on one foot.

GOAL 4   Rides and steers two-wheel bicycle

CRITERION   While sitting on a two-wheel bicycle, child pedals forward and steers bicycle at least 20 feet.

Objective 4.1   Pedals and steers two-wheel bicycle with training wheels

CRITERION   While sitting on a two-wheel bicycle with training wheels with both feet on pedals, child pedals bicycle forward and steers for at least 10 feet.

AEPS™

Adaptive Area
Three to Six Years

LIST OF AEPS TEST ITEMS

Adaptive

NOTE

Parental and cultural values have an effect on what skills a child learns and in what order the skills are learned. Toilet training, the introduction of a variety of food types, use of eating utensils, and personal cleanliness are areas that may differ across cultures and families. While acknowledging these differences, the interventionist should help the child to acquire behaviors (e.g., eating with a fork rather than fingers, wiping nose on tissue rather than shirt sleeve) that are socially acceptable. The lack of socially acceptable skills often results in the exclusion of the child from certain environments.

Adaptive

Mealtime

GOAL 1   Eats and drinks a variety of foods using appropriate utensils with little or no spilling

CRITERION   Child exhibits culturally appropriate social dining skills by performing all of the following activities:

- Puts proper amount of food in mouth, chews with mouth closed, and swallows before taking another bite

- Takes in proper amount of liquid and returns cup to surface

- Eats a variety of food textures

- Selects and eats a variety of food types

- Eats with utensil

NOTE   *If a child's performance on all objectives was scored with a 2, then the goal is scored 2. If a child's performance on the objectives was scored with any combination of a 0, 1, and 2, then the goal is scored 1. If a child's performance on all objectives was scored with a 0, then the goal is scored 0.*

Objective 1.1   Puts proper amount of food in mouth, chews with mouth closed, swallows before taking another bite

CRITERION   Child puts appropriate amount of food in mouth (i.e., does not overfill mouth), chews with mouth closed, and swallows before taking another bite.

Objective 1.2   Takes in proper amount of liquid and returns cup to surface

CRITERION   Child takes in appropriate amount of liquid from child-size cup without spilling and returns cup to table at least once before emptying cup.

Objective 1.3   Eats a variety of food textures

CRITERION   Child eats foods of different textures including:

- Semi-solid foods (applesauce, yogurt)

- Soft foods (bananas, cooked vegetables, macaroni)

- Chewy foods (meats, dried fruits)

- Hard foods (apples, raw vegetables, pretzels)

Objective 1.4   Selects and eats a variety of food types

CRITERION   Child selects and eats a variety of foods from different food groups (e.g., dairy, meat, fruit, vegetables, bread).

Objective 1.5   Eats with utensils

CRITERION   The child eats by spearing with fork and scooping with spoon or other culturally appropriate utensils (e.g., chopsticks), bringing food to mouth with minimal spilling. Child chooses appropriate utensil (e.g., spoon for soup, fork for meat).

GOAL 2   Prepares and serves food

CRITERION   Child performs the following activities prior to eating:

- Prepares food for eating

- Uses knife to spread food

- Pours liquid into a variety of containers

- Serves food with utensil

NOTE   *If a child's performance on all objectives was scored with a 2, then the goal is scored 2. If a child's performance on the objectives was scored with any combination of a 0, 1, and 2, then the goal is scored 1. If a child's performance on all objectives was scored with a 0, then the goal is scored 0.*

Objective 2.1   Prepares food for eating

CRITERION   Child prepares food for eating by removing inedible parts (e.g., peels skin or shell from food, removes paper wrapping, pulls tab on soft drink can).

Objective 2.2   Uses knife to spread food

CRITERION   Child uses a blunt-edged knife to spread soft, spreadable foods (e.g., margarine, cream cheese, jam) on bread or cracker. The bread or cracker should be covered by the food and be intact after child spreads the food. The food does not have to be spread smoothly.

Adaptive

Objective 2.3   Pours liquid into a variety of containers

CRITERION   Child pours liquid from one container (e.g., pitcher, bottle) into another container (e.g., cup, bowl, glass). Child does not spill liquid and stops pouring at the appropriate time to avoid overfilling container.

Objective 2.4   Serves food with utensil

CRITERION   Child uses a utensil to transfer food from one container to another.

Personal Hygiene

GOAL 1 Carries out all toileting functions

CRITERION Child initiates trip to bathroom, pulls down pants, uses toilet paper, pulls up pants, flushes toilet, washes hands, and remains dry and unsoiled between trips to the bathroom. Occasional reminders are acceptable.

Objective 1.1 Uses toilet paper, flushes toilet, washes hands after using toilet

CRITERION Child completes the following toileting routine: pulls down pants, uses toilet paper after using the toilet, pulls up pants, flushes toilet, and washes hands.

Objective 1.2 Uses toilet

CRITERION Child initiates a trip to the bathroom and uses the toilet or potty chair for urination and bowel movement. Child remains dry and unsoiled between trips to the bathroom. Occasional reminders are acceptable. Child may have assistance with other toileting skills (e.g., pulling pants down and up, washing hands).

Objective 1.3 Indicates need to use toilet

CRITERION Child accurately indicates (e.g., tells, signs, gestures) to an adult the need to use the toilet or potty chair for urination and bowel movement.

GOAL 2 Washes and grooms self

CRITERION Child performs the following washing and grooming activities:

- Uses tissue to clean nose

- Brushes teeth

- Bathes and dries self

- Brushes or combs hair

- Washes and dries face

Adaptive

145

NOTE   *If a child's performance on all objectives was scored*
with a 2, then the goal is scored 2. If a child's perfor-
mance on the objectives was scored with any com-
bination of a 0, 1, and 2, then the goal is scored 1.
If a child's performance on all objectives was scored
with a 0, then the goal is scored 0.

Objective 2.1   Uses tissue to clean nose

CRITERION   Child uses a tissue to blow or wipe nose. Child may
be given assistance to thoroughly clean nose.

Objective 2.2   Brushes teeth

CRITERION   Child puts toothpaste on toothbrush, brushes teeth,
and rinses mouth. Reminders are acceptable (e.g.,
"What should you do next?").

Objective 2.3   Bathes and dries self

CRITERION   Child performs the following bathing routine: removes clothing, gets into tub or shower, uses soap
to clean body, rinses off, obtains towel, dries body,
returns towel to towel rack. Reminders are acceptable and child may be given assistance to thoroughly clean and dry self.

Objective 2.4   Brushes or combs hair

CRITERION   Child uses a brush to brush hair or a comb to comb
hair.

Objective 2.5   Washes and dries face

CRITERION   Child completes face washing and drying routine by
turning faucet on, washing face with soap, rinsing
face, turning faucet off, drying face with towel, and
returning towel to towel rack.

Dressing and Undressing

GOAL 1   Unfastens fasteners on garments

CRITERION   Child uses any functional means to perform all of the following unfastening activities:

- Unfastens buttons/snaps/Velcro fasteners on garments
- Unties string-type fastener
- Unzips zipper

NOTE   *If a child's performance on all objectives was scored with a 2, then the goal is scored 2. If a child's performance on the objectives was scored with any combination of a 0, 1, and 2, then the goal is scored 1. If a child's performance on all objectives was scored with a 0, then the goal is scored 0.*

Objective 1.1   Unfastens buttons/snaps/Velcro fasteners on garments

CRITERION   Child unfastens buttons/snaps/Velcro fasteners on garments (e.g., shirt, dress, pants) when undressing, using any functional means that does not damage clothing or fastener.

Objective 1.2   Unties string-type fastener

CRITERION   Child unties string-type fastener (e.g., shoelace, hood string) when undressing, using any functional means that does not damage clothing or fastener.

Objective 1.3   Unzips zipper

CRITERION   Child unzips and detaches zipper on coat, jacket, or sweater when undressing, using any functional means that does not damage clothing or zipper.

GOAL 2   Selects appropriate clothing and dresses self at designated times

CRITERION   Child selects appropriate clothing (i.e., shorts in summer, sweater in winter, nightgown at bedtime) and dresses self at designated time (e.g., after breakfast). Reminders are acceptable.

Adaptive

147

Objective 2.1   Puts on long pants

CRITERION   Child uses any functional means to put pants over both feet and pull them up to the waist. Adult may fasten fasteners.

Objective 2.2   Puts on front-opening garment

CRITERION   Child uses any functional means to put on front-opening garment (e.g., blouse, shirt, coat).

Objective 2.3   Puts on pullover garment

CRITERION   Child uses any functional means to put on pullover garment (e.g., T-shirt, dress, sweater).

Objective 2.4   Puts on shoes

CRITERION   Child uses any functional means to put shoes on both feet. Adult may tie shoes.

Objective 2.5   Puts on underpants, shorts, or skirt

CRITERION   Child uses any functional means to pull underpants, shorts, or skirt over feet and up to waist. Adult may fasten fasteners.

GOAL 3   Fastens fasteners on garments

CRITERION   Child uses any functional means to perform the following:

- Tie string-type fastener

- Fasten buttons/snaps/Velcro fasteners

- Thread and zip zipper

NOTE   *If a child's performance on all objectives was scored with a 2, then the goal is scored 2. If a child's performance on the objectives was scored with any combination of a 0, 1, and 2, then the goal is scored 1. If a child's performance on all objectives was scored with a 0, then the goal is scored 0.*

Objective 3.1   Ties string-type fastener

CRITERION   Child uses any functional means to tie string-type fastener (e.g., shoelace) on own clothing or shoes.

Objective 3.2   Fastens buttons/snaps/Velcro fasteners

CRITERION   Child uses any functional means to fasten buttons/
snaps/Velcro fasteners on own clothing or shoes

Objective 3.3   Threads and zips zipper

CRITERION   Child uses any functional means to thread and zip
zipper on own clothing.

AEPS™

Cognitive Area
Three to Six Years

LIST OF AEPS TEST ITEMS

Cognitive

NOTE

The items in the Cognitive Area were designed to assess the child's cognitive skills as they are used in daily activities. It is important for several reasons to observe the child's behavior across areas. First, traditional developmental categories, such as social, cognitive, and language, are somewhat arbitrary divisions; for example, a child's ability to engage in imaginary play or to participate in classroom activities can be viewed as both social and cognitive behavior. The ability to recall events and information can be viewed as social, cognitive, or communicative behavior.

The second reason to observe a child's behavior across areas is that behavior may be interdependent across areas; for example, a child's ability to follow directions in correct sequence (as in Strand C: Sequencing) is dependent on the child's understanding of verbal instructions. A child's ability to give a reason for an inference or to make a prediction about future events (as in Strand E: Problem Solving) is dependent on the child's expressive communication skills. If a child is unable to perform a given task, then the interventionist should ask, *Is there some other behavior that is absent from the child's repertoire that prevents the child from demonstrating this behavior?*

Young children learning English at the same time that they are learning another language may learn vocabulary to label concepts in both languages. The most accurate measure of conceptual development is to assess the number of concepts learned, rather than the number of vocabulary words used; for example, if a child uses the words "rojo" and "red" interchangeably, then it should be counted as only one color concept, whereas use of "azul" for blue and "rojo" for red should be counted as two separate concepts.

Phonological awareness refers to the ability to hear, compare, contrast, and evaluate the sounds of a language separate from the meaning of words. Rhyming and identifying same and different sounds are examples of phonological skills. Phonological skills are generally acquired during the preschool years and are predictive of competent reading skills in first and second grade. The acquisition of early decoding skills (associating specific sounds with the appropriate letter of the alphabet) also improves phonological skills, so the phonological awareness objectives under Strand H: Goal 1 should not be considered strict prerequisites to the early reading skills in Goals 2 and 3. The goals for letter–sound associations and sight word reading should be considered appropriate for any child who understands the basic print concepts contained in Birth to Three, Cognitive Area, Strand G: Goals 3, 4, and 6.

Cognitive

Concepts

GOAL 1   Demonstrates understanding of color, shape, and size concepts

CRITERION   Child follows directions; answers questions; or identifies objects, people, or events that describe color, shape, and size. Samples of terms for these concepts are described in the underlying objectives.

NOTE   *If a child's performance on all objectives was scored with a 2, then the goal is scored 2. If a child's performance on the objectives was scored with any combination of a 0, 1, and 2, then the goal is scored 1. If a child's performance on all objectives was scored with a 0, then the goal is scored 0.*

Objective 1.1   Demonstrates understanding of eight different colors

CRITERION   Child follows directions; answers questions; or identifies objects, people, or events using at least eight different terms that describe color (e.g., child selects a blue cup at snack time and says, "I want the blue cup"; child says, "Look at my purple coat," when getting coat to go outside; child selects the red paint in response to direction, "Get the red paint"). Terms may include, but are not limited to, the following:

red	blue	orange	pink
yellow	black	purple	gray
green	white	brown	

Objective 1.2   Demonstrates understanding of five different shapes

CRITERION   Child follows directions, answers questions, or identifies objects using at least five different terms that describe shape (e.g., while playing with form boards, child finds the circle and gives it to adult in response to adult's request, "Find a circle"; while gluing triangles on paper, child says, "This triangle is the cat head"). Terms may include, but are not limited to, the following:

circle	triangle	diamond
square	rectangle	star

Objective 1.3 Demonstrates understanding of six different size concepts

CRITERION   Child follows directions, answers questions, or identifies objects or people using at least six different terms that describe size (e.g., while building with blocks of various sizes, child hands adult a small block in response to adult's request to "Give me a small one"; child selects a large car from a group of cars, places a doll in the car, and says, "He wants to ride in the big car"). Terms may include, but are not limited to, the following:

big	thick	small	skinny	chubby
tall	thin	short	tiny	itsy bitsy
little	fat	large	gigantic	long

GOAL 2   Demonstrates understanding of qualitative and quantitative concepts

CRITERION   Child follows directions; answers questions; or identifies objects, people, or events using different terms that describe quality and quantity. Samples of terms for these concepts are described in the underlying objectives.

NOTE   *If a child's performance on all objectives was scored with a 2, then the goal is scored 2. If a child's performance on the objectives was scored with any combination of a 0, 1, and 2, then the goal is scored 1. If a child's performance on all objectives was scored with a 0, then the goal is scored 0.*

Objective 2.1 Demonstrates understanding of 10 different qualitative concepts

CRITERION   Child follows directions; answers questions; or identifies objects, people, or events using at least 10 different terms that describe quality (e.g., while carrying a full basket of toys, the child says, "This is heavy"; child selects the red block from a group of yellow blocks in response to adult's direction, "Find the one that is different"; child points to spilled paint and says, "It's messy and dirty"). Terms may include, but are not limited to, the following:

hot	hard	light	cold	different	clean
soft	same	loud	sour	quiet	dirty
good	rough	heavy	wet	slow	
bad	smooth	dry	sweet	fast	

Cognitive

Objective 2.2   Demonstrates understanding of eight different quantitative concepts

CRITERION   Child follows directions, answers questions, or identifies objects or events using at least eight different terms that describe quantity (e.g., at snack time, child takes several raisins and says, "I have a lot of raisins"; on direction to put away all the blocks, child puts all the blocks in the storage bin). Terms may include, but are not limited to, the following:

all	many	none	full	more	few
less	empty	lots	some	any	each

GOAL 3   Demonstrates understanding of spatial and temporal relations concepts

CRITERION   Child follows directions, answers questions, or identifies objects or events using different terms that describe spatial relations and temporal relations. Samples of terms for these concepts are described in the underlying objectives

NOTE   *If a child's performance on all objectives was scored with a 2, then the goal is scored 2. If a child's performance on the objectives was scored with any combination of a 0, 1, and 2, then the goal is scored 1. If a child's performance on all objectives was scored with a 0, then the goal is scored 0.*

Objective 3.1   Demonstrates understanding of 12 different spatial relations concepts

CRITERION   Child follows directions; answers questions; or identifies objects, people, or events using at least 12 different terms that describe spatial relations (e.g., when lining up to go for a walk, the line leader says, "I am first; you have to get behind me"; child puts crayons in box in response to adult's direction, "Put the crayons in the box"; child follows directions to stand next to the teacher). Terms may include, but are not limited to, the following:

into	back	front	behind	under
here	middle	last	in back of	bottom
beside	down	up	in front of	on
next to	between	there	first	

Objective 3.2   **Demonstrates understanding of seven different temporal relations concepts**

CRITERION   Child follows directions, answers questions, or identifies events using at least seven different terms that describe temporal relations (e.g., child gives appropriate response to adult's question, "What do we do before we have lunch?" ["We wash our hands"]; while building a tower of blocks, child says, "After it gets this big, I'll knock it down," child builds tower to specified height, then knocks it down). Terms may include, but are not limited to, the following:

yesterday	early	before	if-then	today
later	after	tomorrow	last	first

Categorizing

GOAL 1 Groups objects, people, or events on the basis of specified criteria

CRITERION Child specifies a criterion and places all objects into groups according to that criterion (e.g., category, function, physical attribute). When playing with group of miniature objects, child separates objects into groups of people, animals, and vehicles; child separates objects according to color. Adult may provide general cue (e.g., "Put all the ones together that go together").

Objective 1.1 Groups objects, people, or events on the basis of category

CRITERION Child places all objects into groups according to some categorical criterion (e.g., food, animals, clothing). Adult may provide categories (e.g., "Put the food on the table and the clothing in the box").

Objective 1.2 Groups objects on the basis of function

CRITERION Child places all objects into groups according to function (e.g., things to eat with, things that go in water). Before water play activity, child chooses from a group of toys all those appropriate for water play.

Objective 1.3 Groups objects on the basis of physical attribute

CRITERION Child places all objects into groups according to some physical attribute (e.g., color, shape, size, texture). When playing with colored blocks, child separates them into groups according to color; after playing with toy vehicles, child puts large vehicles on one shelf and small vehicles on another.

Sequencing

GOAL 1 Follows directions of three or more related steps that are not routinely given

CRITERION   Child responds with actions in correct sequence to a functional three-step direction (i.e., within context) that is not part of the typical routine. During gross motor activity, adult gestures and tells child, "Run to the bench, pick up the ball, and then run to the slide." Contextual cues such as gestures may be given.

Objective 1.1 Follows directions of three or more related steps that are routinely given

CRITERION   Child responds with actions in correct sequence to a functional three-step direction (i.e., within context) that is part of the usual routine. After being outside, adult gestures and tells child, "Take off your coat, hang it up, and then wash your hands." Contextual cues such as gestures may be given.

GOAL 2 Places objects in series according to length or size

CRITERION   Child places three or more objects in a series according to length or size (e.g., child puts books on shelf in order of height; child stacks dishes with largest on bottom and others progressively smaller). Child may correct self.

Objective 2.1 Fits one ordered set of objects to another

CRITERION   Child matches two related sets of two or more objects by assigning each object from one set to its matching object from the other set (e.g., child fits a set of two different-size lids to correct bowls; child fits a set of three different bolts to correct nuts). Child may correct self.

GOAL 3 Retells event in sequence

CRITERION   Child retells a sequence of at least three events verbally, through gestures and demonstration or by arranging pictures in correct sequence (e.g., adult tells three-part story and asks child to retell story, child gestures, tells story verbally, or arranges story pictures in correct sequence to retell story; child tells caregiver about a field trip earlier in the day by saying "We went on the bus to the pumpkin farm; first we picked out our pumpkins and then we ate lunch" [Alternately, the child may arrange photographs of the trip in correct sequence.])

Objective 3.1   Completes sequence of familiar story or event

CRITERION   Child responds appropriately to question about sequence of story or event verbally, through gestures and demonstration, or by arranging pictures in correct sequence (e.g., when telling story, child responds appropriately to adult's question, "Then what happened?"; child responds with appropriate motor action to adult's question, "What do you do next?"; child chooses correct picture to complete sequence in response to adult's request, "Pick the one that goes here").

Recalling Events

GOAL 1   Recalls events that occurred on same day, without contextual cues

CRITERION   Without contextual cues and at least 30 minutes after occurrence of event, child spontaneously and accurately relates (e.g., tells, demonstrates) an event that occurred on the same day. At end of school day, adult asks, "What did you make in art today?" Art project and materials are not present in environment. Child responds by accurately telling what was made during art activity. Child says, "I painted a picture of a dog" or pantomimes making a hat and putting it on.

Objective 1.1   Recalls events that occurred on same day, with contextual cues

CRITERION   With contextual cues (i.e., being in same setting or with same object) and at least 30 minutes after occurrence of event, child spontaneously and accurately relates (e.g., tells, demonstrates) an event that occurred on the same day (e.g., during circle time in classroom, adult asks, with toys present in the environment, "What did you do to have fun today?", child responds by saying, "I played with the dolls," which had occurred prior to circle time).

Objective 1.2   Recalls events immediately after they occur

CRITERION   Spontaneously or on request, child accurately relates (e.g., tells, demonstrates) events that occurred immediately before (e.g., child washes hands, walks out of bathroom, and tells adult, "I washed my hands").

Cognitive

163

Problem Solving

GOAL 1   Evaluates solutions to problems

CRITERION   Spontaneously or on request, child indicates (e.g., tells, demonstrates) why a particular solution to a problem within context would or would not work (e.g., when asked, "What could we use to stick these together?", the child produces reasoned responses ["We could chew up some gum if there's no glue"; "Water won't work; it isn't sticky"]; child stands on chair to reach toys on shelf and says to adult, "This chair is too small. I can't reach," and goes to find a taller chair).

Objective 1.1   Suggests acceptable solutions to problems

CRITERION   Spontaneously or on request, child indicates (e.g., tells, demonstrates) acceptable solutions to problems (e.g., child who is having difficulty cutting says, "You hold the paper for me," points to a different pair of scissors when asked, "What can we try?"). General cues may be given by adult (e.g. "What can we do?" "What can you try?").

Objective 1.2   Identifies means to goal

CRITERION   Spontaneously or on request, child names or selects appropriate/functional means to goal when problem and solution have been identified (e.g., child brings a large empty container in response to adult's request, "Find something for carrying the blocks"; child points to chair in response to adult's request, "Find something to stand on that will help you reach the toy").

GOAL 2   Makes statements and appropriately answers questions that require reasoning about objects, situations, or people

CRITERION   Child makes statements and appropriately answers questions that require the child to do the following:

- Give reason for inference

- Make prediction about future or hypothetical event

- Give possible cause of some event

NOTE *If a child's performance on all objectives was scored with a 2, then the goal is scored 2. If a child's performance on the objectives was scored with any combination of a 0, 1, and 2, then the goal is scored 1. If a child's performance on all objectives was scored with a 0, then the goal is scored 0.*

Objective 2.1   Gives reason for inference

CRITERION   Spontaneously or on request, child gives plausible reason for making inference (e.g., child says, "She is sad," and adult asks, "How do you know that the girl is sad?", child answers, "Because she's crying"; child looks out the window and says, "I think it's raining, because he has an umbrella"; "I need my warm coat, it's snowing").

Objective 2.2   Makes prediction about future or hypothetical events

CRITERION   Spontaneously or on request, child makes a plausible prediction about future or hypothetical events that take place within context (e.g., adult who is reading unfamiliar story pauses and asks child, "What do you think will happen?", child makes plausible prediction.)

Objective 2.3   Gives possible cause for some event

CRITERION   Spontaneously or on request, child tells possible cause for observed event (e.g., child tells plausible cause for event in response to adult's question, "Why do you think she is crying?" ["Because she fell down"; "Maybe somebody broke her doll"]).

Cognitive

Play

GOAL 1   Engages in cooperative, imaginary play

CRITERION   Child engages in the following play behaviors with peers:

- Enacts roles or identities

- Plans and acts out recognizable event, theme, or storyline

- Uses imaginary props

NOTE   *If a child's performance on all objectives was scored with a 2, then the goal is scored 2. If a child's performance on the objectives was scored with any combination of a 0, 1, and 2, then the goal is scored 1. If a child's performance on all objectives was scored with a 0, then the goal is scored 0.*

Objective 1.1   Enacts roles or identities

CRITERION   Child assumes recognizable roles or identities when playing with peers by announcing the role or by changing voice, manner, or behavior to indicate an identity (e.g., child says, "I'll be the bus driver," sits in front seat of pretend bus, and tells other children in an adult voice, "Please sit down and be quiet while I'm driving").

Objective 1.2   Plans and acts out recognizable event, theme, or storyline

CRITERION   Child uses words and actions to plan and enact a recognizable event, theme, or storyline, alone or with peers (e.g., child says, "I'll be the mommy and I'm going to the store," child puts on hat and takes purse, pretends to go to the store, comes home, and cooks dinner).

Objective 1.3   Uses imaginary props

CRITERION   Child plays using imaginary props, alone or with peers (e.g., child gallops around room pretending to hold reins and says, "Giddy up, horsie, go fast"; child pretends to feed doll with imaginary spoon).

GOAL 2 Engages in games with rules

CRITERION Child engages in games with rules by

- Maintaining participation

- Conforming to game rules

NOTE *If a child's performance on all objectives was scored with a 2, then the goal is scored 2. If a child's performance on the objectives was scored with any combination of a 0, 1, and 2, then the goal is scored 1. If a child's performance on all objectives was scored with a 0, then the goal is scored 0.*

Objective 2.1 Maintains participation

CRITERION Child continues to participate in organized game until completion of game (e.g., child rolls ball back and forth to adult until adult says, "It's time for snack"). Group directions may be provided by adult.

Objective 2.2 Conforms to game rules

CRITERION Child follows rules in organized games (e.g., child waits for turn, follows appropriate sequence of steps in game, and knows beginning and end of game). Group directions may be provided by adult.

Cognitive

Premath

GOAL 1 Counts at least 20 objects

CRITERION Child counts 20 or more objects, assigning numbers to objects in the correct order, and counting each object only once (e.g., child correctly counts 22 of 25 crayons, moving each one to a pile on the side of the table as it is counted; the child may make mistakes above 20 and still be scored a 2 on this item; for example, the child counts crayons correctly to 22, but then counts 20, 21, 22 again for the remaining three crayons). The child touches, points to, or moves each object while counting.

Objective 1.1 Counts at least 10 objects

CRITERION Child counts between 10 and 20 objects, assigning numbers to objects in the correct order, and counting each object only once (e.g., child correctly counts 13 of 15 chairs, pointing to each one in turn while counting; the child may make mistakes above 10 and still be scored a 2 on this item; for example, the child counts chairs correctly to 13, but then counts 16, 17 for the remaining two chairs). The child touches, points to, or moves each object while counting.

Objective 1.2 Counts three objects

CRITERION Child counts at least three and up to nine objects, assigning numbers to objects in the correct order, and counting each object only once (e.g., child counts four of six puppies, touching each one in turn while counting; the child may make mistakes between three and nine and still be scored a 2 on this item; for example, the child correctly counts four puppies but then touches two of the same puppies again and skips five, ending up at seven but having missed two puppies). The child touches, points to, or moves each object while counting.

GOAL 2 Demonstrates understanding of printed numerals

CRITERION Child correctly discriminates numerals from letters (e.g., child correctly uses the word *number* only when identifying numerals and never for letters), uses number symbols to represent quantity (e.g., child says, "There are four apples"), and uses numbers as identifiers for daily events, objects, and personal information (e.g., child says, "I am 5 years old"; "There is Room 6").

Objective 2.1   Labels printed numerals up to 10

CRITERION   Child associates number words with the correct printed numeral (e.g., child says "one" when presented with the numeral 1, "two" when presented with the numeral 2, and so forth up to 10).

Objective 2.2   Recognizes printed numerals

CRITERION   Child discriminates numbers from letters and other symbols by matching and sorting printed numerals from letters and finding numbers when asked (e.g., when asked to find something with numbers, the child identifies a calendar, the room number over the door, the house number).

Cognitive

Phonological Awareness and Emergent Reading

STRAND
H

GOAL 1   Demonstrates phonological awareness skills

CRITERION   Child demonstrates awareness of the component sounds of his or her primary language by

- Rhyming words (e.g., child can say *hat, cat, bat* when asked to rhyme words)

- Segmenting sentences and words (e.g., child can divide words into component sounds/syllables or sentences into words)

- Blending sounds into words (e.g., child says, "C-A-T is cat")

- Identifying same and different sounds at beginning and end of words (e.g., given the word "snake," the child can say words that start with the /s/ sound and end with the /s/ sound)

NOTE   *If a child's performance on all objectives was scored with a 2, then the goal is scored 2. If a child's performance on the objectives was scored with any combination of a 0, 1, and 2, then the goal is scored 1. If a child's performance on all objectives was scored with a 0, then the goal is scored 0.*

Objective 1.1   Uses rhyming skills

CRITERION   Child uses rhyming skills by recognizing words that do and do not rhyme and filling in missing words in rhymes (e.g., child says, "boy–girl" do not rhyme and says "bear–chair" do rhyme; adult asks for a word that rhymes with "dog" and the child says, "frog" or for a word that rhymes with "mat" and child says, "pat"). The word produced can be a nonsense word if it rhymes.

Objective 1.2   Segments sentences and words

CRITERION   Child identifies each word in multiple four- to six-word utterances by saying each word separately and in the correct sequence and identify each separate sound or syllable of words (e.g., child says, "We-want-to-go-outside" when an adult says the sentence and asks the child, "Can you say each word by itself?"; adult says, "Tell me the sounds in the word *hop*." The child says, "h – o – p," with each sound identifiable and in the correct sequence).

Objective 1.3 Blends single sounds and syllables

CRITERION Child blends two to three syllables into a word and three to four separate sounds into words, when the sounds and syllables are provided slowly and in the correct order (e.g., adult says, "Tell me what word these sounds make: "b – a – t" and the child says, "bat"; adult says, "bi – cy – cle" and child says, "bi-cycle"; adult says "ba – na – na" and child says "banana").

Objective 1.4 Identifies same and different sounds at the beginning and end of words

CRITERION Child identifies same and different sounds in words by recognizing words with the same/different initial and ending sounds and producing words with same initial sounds (e.g., adult says, "Tell me some other words that start with the same sound as "bear," and the child says "ball," "bagel," "baby"; adult says, "Tell me some words that start with different sounds than "bear" and child says, "cow" and "dog").

GOAL 2 Uses letter–sound associations to sound out and write words

CRITERION Child uses at least 20 individual letter sounds to sound out words and write words (e.g., child sounds out and/or writes the word "map" by blending the sounds m – a – p; inaccurate pronunciations and invented spellings are acceptable, as long as correct letter-sound associations are used in attempts to read and write; child might read "soap" as "so – ap" or write party as "p – r – t – e"). The child's attempts to sound out words do not need to be completely accurate, and invented spellings are acceptable.

NOTE *If a child's performance on all objectives was scored with a 2, then the goal is scored 2. If a child's performance on the objectives was scored with any combination of a 0, 1, and 2, then the goal is scored 1. If a child's performance on all objectives was scored with a 0, then the goal is scored 0.*

Objective 2.1 Writes words using letter sounds

CRITERION Child assigns appropriate sounds to letters as he or she attempts to write words (e.g., child might spell "house" as h – o – w – s). Invented spellings are acceptable, as are any sounds that can reasonably be associated with letters.

Cognitive

Objective 2.2   Sounds out words

CRITERION   Child produces correct sounds in sequence as he or she attempts to sound out words (e.g., child might sound out "boat " as "bow – at"; child looks at a restroom sign and sounds out "B – o – y – s, boys"). The child does not actually need to decode the word correctly as long as plausible sounds are assigned to each letter.

Objective 2.3   Produces correct sounds for letters

CRITERION   Given books, letter puzzles, alphabet cards, or similar materials, the child matches sounds to printed letters by producing correct sounds for at least 15 letters.

GOAL 3   Reads words by sight

CRITERION   Spontaneously or on request, child reads at least five common words by sight (e.g., child says, "That says 'Stop'" after seeing a stop sign while riding in car; says, "Men" after seeing a restroom sign). One of the words may be the child's first name.

Objective 3.1   Identifies letter names

CRITERION   Spontaneously or on request, child names at least 20 letters of the alphabet (e.g., adult shows child printed letters and asks, "Can you name any of these letters?").

AEPS™

Social-Communication Area
Three to Six Years

LIST OF AEPS TEST ITEMS

3.4   Asks "why," "who," and "how" questions

3.5   Asks "what" and "where" questions

3.6   Asks questions using rising inflections

4.1   Uses subject pronouns

4.2   Uses object pronouns

4.3   Uses possessive pronouns

4.4   Uses indefinite pronouns

4.5   Uses demonstrative pronouns

5.1   Uses adjectives

5.2   Uses adjectives to make comparisons

5.3   Uses adverbs

5.4   Uses prepositions

5.5   Uses conjunctions

5.6   Uses articles

NOTE

The Social-Communication Area was designed to assess the child's language and communication skills as they are used in community and home activities, conversations, and social interactions. Items in this area evaluate social-communication interactions, such as the child's use of words and of conversational rules and grammatical structures.

The user is reminded that many skills assessed in the Social-Communication Area may also be dependent on skills assessed in the Cognitive and Social Areas; for example, a child's ability to name and identify colors (skills included in the Cognitive Area) is dependent on the child's understanding of verbal instructions or questions such as, "Show me which one is green" or "What color is this?" If a child is unable to perform a given task, then the interventionist should ask, "Is there another behavior absent from the child's repertoire that prevents the child from demonstrating this behavior?"

Young children acquiring more than one language simultaneously initially learn vocabulary without distinguishing between languages. The number of words in a child's vocabulary, therefore, should be counted as the *total*

Social-Communication

number of words or word approximations the child is using in *both* languages. This principle holds for children learning English as a second language, as well as for children from bilingual and multilingual homes. Typically developing youngsters do not reliably and consistently sort languages into separate systems until they acquire cognitive skills of categorization and classification, usually after the third birthday.

Young children from bilingual homes or who are learning English as a second language should always be assessed for comprehension in both languages and, if possible, in multiple settings. Children may use the family's native language predominantly at home and English at a center-based program, even if they have more sophisticated skills in the native language. An accurate measure of comprehension, therefore, includes presenting AEPS Test items in any language to which the child is regularly exposed.

Two additional forms, the Social-Communication Observation Form and the Social-Communication Summary Form, are used for the purpose of collecting, recording, and analyzing the child's social-communication behavior. Both of these forms are contained in Appendix C of Volume 1 and directions for using the forms are contained in Chapter 3 of Volume 1. These forms, or similar forms, are strongly recommended for use in scoring the Social-Communication Area. Information on collecting data in the Social-Communication Area is provided at the end of this area.

CAUTION

Some children have difficulty with production of the speech sounds of language (i.e., articulation delay). The AEPS Test does not provide a formalized procedure for assessing speech skills. Consult a qualified specialist to assess concerns in the area of articulation delays. The interventionist is encouraged to share the AEPS Test results with the specialist, as it will provide valuable information regarding the child's speech skills within conversation.

Social-Communicative Interactions

GOAL 1   Uses words, phrases, or sentences to inform, direct, ask questions, and express anticipation, imagination, affect, and emotions

CRITERION   Child uses words, phrases, or sentences to do the following:

- Express anticipated outcomes
- Describe pretend objects, events, or people
- Label own or others' affect/emotions
- Describe past events
- Make commands to and requests of others
- Obtain information
- Inform

Errors in syntax are acceptable.

NOTE   *If a child's performance on all objectives was scored with a 2, then the goal is scored 2. If a child's performance on the objectives was scored with any combination of a 0, 1, and 2, then the goal is scored 1. If a child's performance on all objectives was scored with a 0, then the goal is scored 0.*

Objective 1.1   Uses words, phrases, or sentences to express anticipated outcomes

CRITERION   Child uses words, phrases, or sentences to express anticipated outcome (e.g., child says, "Look out," when an object falls from the table; child predicts the ending of a familiar story, child says, "Santa will come on my roof at Christmas"; while reading a story, adult pauses and says, "Uh-oh, I wonder what happens next," child says, "I think the giant will wake up"; adult asks, "What will you do this weekend?", child says, "My daddy is going to take me fishing"). Errors in syntax are acceptable.

Objective 1.2   Uses words, phrases, or sentences to describe pretend objects, events, or people

CRITERION   Child uses words, phrases, or sentences to tell about pretend objects, events, or people (e.g., child says, "I

177

am Superman"; child says, "Let's build a campfire. You go get some wood," and acts out a camping scenario; adult says, "Let's play going to the beach," child says, "I'll get the towels and suntan lotion," and gathers pretend objects; child says, "Let's pretend this is a hospital. I'll be the doctor. Who do you want to be?"). Errors in syntax are acceptable.

Objective 1.3   Uses words, phrases, or sentences to label own or others' affect/emotions

CRITERION   Child uses words, phrases, or sentences to label own or others' affect/emotions (e.g., child begins crying and says, "I don't like that"; child watches an adult laugh and says, "You're happy"; adult says, "The boy can't find his puppy. I wonder how he feels?", child says, "I think he's sad" or "He's sad"). Errors in syntax are acceptable.

Objective 1.4   Uses words, phrases, or sentences to describe past events

CRITERION   Child uses words, phrases, or sentences to describe actions and events that occurred in the immediate and distant past (e.g., child says, "The bad guy chased him and he fell down" when telling about a movie previously viewed; child says, "I made a hat" when telling parent about an earlier art activity; adult asks child what was done in school, child says, "I painted a picture of a boat"). Errors in syntax are acceptable.

Objective 1.5   Uses words, phrases, or sentences to make commands to and requests of others

CRITERION   Child uses words, phrases, or sentences to make commands to and requests of others (e.g., child says, "Give me the red one"; When playing on a swing set, child says, "Push me"). Errors in syntax are acceptable.

Objective 1.6   Uses words, phrases, or sentences to obtain information

CRITERION   Child uses words, phrases, or sentences to obtain information (e.g., child can't locate coat and asks, "My coat?" [with rising intonation]; child watches peer eating and says, "That your cookie?"; child asks classroom teachers, "Mommy comes back?") Errors in syntax are acceptable.

Objective 1.7   Uses words, phrases, or sentences to inform

CRITERION   Child uses words, phrases, or sentences to describe objects, actions, and events and to relay plans, intentions, and experiences to others (e.g., child calls to parent, "I'm going outside"; child approaches a peer and says, "I have red shoes"; child points to truck and says, "That's my daddy's truck"; child is drawing and adult says, "Oh, that's a nice picture" and child says, "It's my house"; adult asks, "What color do you want?" and child says, "Red"). Errors in syntax are acceptable.

GOAL 2   Uses conversational rules

CRITERION   Child uses conversational rules to initiate and maintain communicative exchanges for two or more consecutive exchanges. An exchange includes a response from both the child and another person. Conversational rules include the following:

- Alternating between speaker/listener role

- Responding to topic changes

- Asking questions for clarification

- Responding to contingent questions

- Initiating context-relevant topics

- Responding to others' topic initiations

NOTE   *If a child's performance on all objectives was scored with a 2, then the goal is scored 2. If a child's performance on the objectives was scored with any combination of a 0, 1, and 2, then the goal is scored 1. If a child's performance on all objectives was scored with a 0, then the goal is scored 0.*

Objective 2.1   Alternates between speaker/listener role

CRITERION   Child uses appropriate responses in conversation to alternate between speaker/listener role (e.g., child pauses after making a comment or asking a question and looks toward communicative partner; child asks, "Where's my book?", mother says, "Here," child asks, "Where?").

Objective 2.2   Responds to topic changes initiated by others

CRITERION   Child responds to conversational topic changes initiated by others with a comment, answer, or question related to the new topic (e.g., child says, "I want to play outside some more," and adult says, "We need to go inside now to fix a special snack," child responds, "What is it?"; child says, "I like to play with cars"; adult says, "Look, it's raining," child responds, "I need my rain boots"; during classroom circle activity, child says, "I like the farm animals"; adult says, "It's time for snack," child responds, "Juice and crackers").

Objective 2.3   Asks questions for clarification

CRITERION   Child indicates a need for clarification (i.e., repetition, elaboration, confirmation) by commenting or questioning during communicative exchanges (e.g., child says, "What?" when child does not understand what another person said; child asks, "What one?" when unsure about which object was indicated by another; adult points to a shelf of dolls and asks, "Can you give me the doll?", child asks, "Which one?").

Objective 2.4   Responds to contingent questions

CRITERION   Child supplies relevant information following another person's request for clarification, repetition, elaboration, or confirmation of child's previous statement (e.g., child says, "They threw it," adult asks, "Who threw it?", child answers, "Rachel. Rachel threw it"; child says, "These shoes," adult asks, "Are those your shoes?", child nods affirmatively and says, "Yep"; adult asks, "Why do you have your coat on?", child says, "It's cold"; child says, "I'm going shopping with my mom after school," adult says, "What are you going to buy?", child says, "Cereal").

Objective 2.5   Initiates context-relevant topics

CRITERION   Child initiates topics relevant to the situation or communicative partner (e.g., child sees peer with crayons and says, "I want the red one"; child sees adult wearing sunglasses and says, "You have glasses").

Objective 2.6   Responds to others' topic initiations

CRITERION   Child responds to another's conversation with a related topic, including an acknowledgment of another's statement, an answer to a question, a request for clarification, or a related comment (e.g., adult says, "It's time to get your coats and hats and line up at the door," child says, "Okay"; adult comments, "You have new shoes on today," child says, "My mommy got them at the store"; adult asks, "What did you do?", child answers, "Fall down"; adult approaches child and says, "Your mom brought you to school today," child says, "Mommy doesn't work today").

GOAL 3   Establishes and varies social-communicative roles

CRITERION   Child changes form, length, and grammatical complexity of phrases and sentences according to the listener's needs and social role (e.g., child says, "I want some gum" to a parent but uses polite form, "Can I have some gum please?" with less familiar adults; child uses shorter and less complex sentences to ask a younger child, "Want a cookie?").

Objective 3.1   Varies voice to impart meaning

CRITERION   Child uses voice pitch (i.e., high, low) and intensity (i.e., loud, soft) appropriate to the situation, listener, and communicative meaning (e.g., child shouts when playing but whispers after noticing father is sleeping; child uses higher pitch and less intensity when speaking to infants; child raises pitch at the end of sentences that are questions).

Objective 3.2   Uses socially appropriate physical orientation

CRITERION   Child looks toward speaker's face and establishes appropriate physical proximity and body posture in relation to others during communicative exchange (e.g., when child's name is called, child turns and looks to locate the speaker; child looks at and leans toward a friend who wants to tell a secret).

Social-Communication

Production of Words, Phrases, and Sentences

GOAL 1   Uses verbs

CRITERION   Child uses the following verb forms:

- Auxiliary

- Copula verb "to be"

- Third person singular

- Irregular past tense

- Regular past tense

- Present progressive "ing"

NOTE   *If a child's performance on all objectives was scored with a 2, then the goal is scored 2. If a child's performance on the objectives was scored with any combination of a 0, 1, and 2, then the goal is scored 1. If a child's performance on all objectives was scored with a 0, then the goal is scored 0.*

Objective 1.1   Uses auxiliary verbs

CRITERION   Child uses an appropriate form of the following auxiliary (helping) verbs in combination with other verbs:

- To be (e.g., "She is running," "She's jumping," "They were throwing rocks")

- To want (e.g., "I want to go")

- Will (e.g., "You will fall," "They won't tell her," "She would go")

- Can (e.g., "I could eat that," "We can go," "I can't swim")

- To do (e.g., "I do want that," "They don't go to school," "She doesn't like milk")

- Shall (e.g., "He should take a nap")

- May (e.g., "He might not like it")

- Better (e.g., "You better do it")

- To have (e.g., "Do I have to do it?")

The number of forms the child uses is less important than the child's ability to use a form appropriate to the grammatical and semantic context of the sentence (e.g., adult pushes car along floor and child says, "I want to do it"; adult puts doll in bed and asks, "What is the baby doing?", child says, "He is sleeping"; adult gets coat and says, "What should we do?", child says, "We better go"; adult observes child and says, "What are you doing?", child says, "I'm cutting this").

Objective 1.2   Uses copula verb "to be"

CRITERION   Child uses an appropriate form of the verb "to be" to link a subject noun to a predicate (e.g., child says, "I'm happy," "They are sick," "He wasn't at home," "She's funny"; when playing with blocks, adult selects a large block and says, "This one is big," adult hands a small block to child and child says, "This one is littler"; adult looks around and asks, "Where are the blocks?" and child says, "They're on the shelf"; adult asks, "How do you feel today?" and child says, "I am tired").

Objective 1.3   Uses third person singular verb forms

CRITERION   Child uses appropriate regular and irregular third person singular verb forms (e.g., has, was, does, is, come, went, ran, drank, ate, wrote; regular third person: child says, "She plays it," "It jumps," "The dog barks"; irregular third person: child says, "She has a bike," "He does not").

Objective 1.4   Uses irregular past tense verbs

CRITERION   Child uses appropriate irregular forms of past tense verbs (e.g., came, ran, fell, broke, sat, went, told, heard, did, ate, woke, made, drank, wrote; child says, "Mommy went to work," "I ran fast"; when adult says, "I had fun on my vacation. I went to see my mother," child says, "I went to my grandma's, and she made some cookies"; teacher asks, "What did you do before you came to school today?", child says, "I woke up, and I ate breakfast").

Objective 1.5   Uses regular past tense verbs

CRITERION   Child uses appropriate regular past tense verbs (i.e., verb plus "ed" ending; e.g., child says, "We walked home," "I washed my hands"; adult asks, "What did you do outside today?", child says, "I played on the swings").

Objective 1.6   Uses present progressive "ing"

CRITERION   Child uses appropriate present progressive verb forms (i.e., verb plus "ing" ending; e.g., child says, "I'm going outside," "Daddy's washing dishes"; adult pretends to feed doll and asks, "What is the baby doing?", child responds, "She's eating").

GOAL 2   Uses noun inflections

CRITERION   Child uses the following noun inflections:

- Possessive "s" (e.g., Susan's)

- Irregular plural (e.g., mice)

- Regular plural (e.g., toys)

NOTE   *If a child's performance on all objectives was scored with a 2, then the goal is scored 2. If a child's performance on the objectives was scored with any combination of a 0, 1, and 2, then the goal is scored 1. If a child's performance on all objectives was scored with a 0, then the goal is scored 0.*

Objective 2.1   Uses possessive "s"

CRITERION   Child uses nouns with an apostrophe "s" to express possession (e.g., "Mom's hat fell off," "Ann's shoes are lost"; teacher passes out art projects, gives child a peer's drawing, and says, "Here is your picture," child says, "This is Jenny's picture, not mine"; Teacher asks, "Whose coat is this," child says, "It's Mary's").

Objective 2.2   Uses irregular plural nouns

CRITERION   Child uses irregular plural noun forms (e.g., mice, leaves, geese, feet, teeth; child says, "Those mice are in the cage," "My teeth are brushed"; adult presents three toy mice and asks child, "What are these?", child says "Mice").

Objective 2.3   Uses regular plural nouns

CRITERION   Child uses regular plural noun forms (i.e., noun plus "s" or "es" ending; e.g., child says, "I see the dogs," "I have two glasses"; adult presents blocks and asks child, "What do you want?", child says, "Blocks, please"; adult says, "I want to light these candles, What do I need?", child responds, "Matches").

GOAL 3   Asks questions

CRITERION   Child uses the following forms to ask questions:

- Yes/no questions

- Questions with inverted auxiliary

- "When" questions

- "Why," "who," and "how" questions

- "What" and "where" questions

- Rising inflection

NOTE   *If a child's performance on all objectives was scored with a 2, then the goal is scored 2. If a child's performance on the objectives was scored with any combination of a 0, 1, and 2, then the goal is scored 1. If a child's performance on all objectives was scored with a 0, then the goal is scored 0.*

Objective 3.1   Asks yes/no questions

CRITERION   Child asks questions that require a yes or no response from the listener (e.g., child asks, "Am I bigger?", "Can I go?"; adult is helping child complete a puzzle, child picks up puzzle piece, points to place on puzzle, asks, "Does this one go here?"; adult says, "I have cookies," child asks, "Chocolate?").

Objective 3.2   Asks questions with inverted auxiliary

CRITERION   Child asks questions by reversing the order of the subject and the auxiliary (helping) verb (i.e., verb precedes the noun; e.g., child asks, "Why can't I go?", "Is he hiding?"; while playing with miniature animals, adult asks child to find animal that hops, child retrieves frog and asks, "Can he hop?"; adult says, "I am going to the store", child says, "Can I go, too?").

Objective 3.3   Asks "when" questions

CRITERION   Child asks questions beginning with the word "when" (e.g., child asks, "When can we do it?", "When will we eat?"; adult plays organized game with a group of children, child asks, "When can I have a turn?"; adult says, "We're going to McDonald's", child asks, "When can we go?").

Objective 3.4   Asks "why," "who," and "how" questions

CRITERION   Child asks questions beginning with the words "why," "who," and "how" (e.g., child asks, "Why did he do that?", "Who is it?", "How do you do that?"; child and adult are playing with dolls, adult says, "We have to take this baby to the doctor," child asks, "Why?"; adult hands telephone to child and says, "It's for you," child asks, "Who is it?"; adult shows child a magic trick, child asks, "How did you do that?").

Objective 3.5   Asks "what" and "where" questions

CRITERION   Child asks questions beginning with the words "what" and "where" (e.g., child asks, "Where is she going?", "Where Mommy going?", "What's that noise?"; adult presents unfamiliar object, child asks, "What is that?"; adult hides object, child asks, "Where is my doll?"; adult says, "Ann is hiding, can you find her?", child asks, "Ann, where are you?").

Objective 3.6   Asks questions using rising inflections

CRITERION   Child asks questions by using a raised pitch at the end of utterances so that the utterances sound like questions (e.g., child asks, "See that airplane?", "Mommy go too?"; adult and child are playing a game, child asks, "My turn?").

GOAL 4   Uses pronouns

CRITERION   Child uses appropriate pronouns to serve the following functions:

- As subjects in phrases or sentences

- As objects in phrases or sentences

- To show possession

- To represent indefinite people and objects

- To identify or point out objects (demonstrative pronouns)

NOTES   *If a child's performance on all objectives was scored with a 2, then the goal is scored 2. If a child's performance on the objectives was scored with any combination of a 0, 1, and 2, then the goal is scored 1. If a child's performance on all objectives was scored with a 0, then the goal is scored 0.*

Objective 4.1 Uses subject pronouns

CRITERION Child uses subject pronouns appropriately as the subject in phrases or sentences (e.g., child asks, "They went home?" "I did it?" "You have ice cream?"; child says, "He is driving fast"; "She is jumping off the boat"; "We are swimming"). The number of different subject pronouns the child uses is less important than the child's ability to use a subject pronoun in the grammatical and semantic context of the sentence. Subject pronouns include the following:

I	he	it	they
you	she	we	

Objective 4.2 Uses object pronouns

CRITERION Child uses object pronouns appropriately as the object (i.e., receives an object or relation) in phrases or sentences (e.g., child says, "John hurt me," "I want you to go," "I gave it to her," "I'll give him some paint," "I'll give her some water," "Give her some paint, too," "Give it to me"). The number of different object pronouns used by the child is less important than the child's ability to use an object pronoun appropriate to the grammatical and semantic context of the sentence. Object pronouns include the following:

me	her	it	them
you	mine	us	

Objective 4.3 Uses possessive pronouns

CRITERION Child uses possessive pronouns appropriately to express possession in phrases or sentences (e.g., child says, "Those are her shoes," "I like his toy better"; adult holds up coat and asks, "Whose is this?", child says, "It's mine"). The number of different possessive pronouns used by the child is less important than the child's ability to use a possessive pronoun appropriate to the grammatical and semantic context of the sentence. Possessive pronouns include the following:

my/mine	his	our/ours	its
your/yours	her/hers	their/theirs	

Objective 4.4 Uses indefinite pronouns

CRITERION Child uses indefinite pronouns appropriately to refer to an unspecified person or object (e.g., child says, "Can't I have some?", "Do you want any?",

"No one wants more," "There's nothing to do"; adult and child are playing with blocks, adult says, "I need a yellow block," child says, "I have some here"). The number of different indefinite pronouns used by the child is less important than the child's ability to use an indefinite pronoun appropriate to the grammatical and semantic context of the sentence. Indefinite pronouns include the following:

all	everything	some	something
nothing	many	more	lots
any	every	anything	none

Objective 4.5   Uses demonstrative pronouns

CRITERION   Child uses demonstrative pronouns appropriately to single out or identify objects (e.g., child says, "I want those," "That's not my coat," "Can I have this cookie?", "These are mine," "That one"). The number of different demonstrative pronouns used by the child is less important than the child's ability to use a demonstrative pronoun appropriate to the grammatical and semantic context of the sentence. Demonstrative pronouns include the following:

| this | these | that | those |

GOAL 5   Uses descriptive words

CRITERION   Child uses descriptive, relational, and functional words as

- Adjectives

- Adverbs

- Prepositions

- Conjunctions

- Articles

NOTE   *If a child's performance on all objectives was scored with a 2, then the goal is scored 2. If a child's performance on the objectives was scored with any combination of a 0, 1, and 2, then the goal is scored 1. If a child's performance on all objectives was scored with a 0, then the goal is scored 0.*

Objective 5.1   Uses adjectives

CRITERION   Child uses adjectives to modify nouns and pronouns (e.g., child says, "My hands are cold," "I want the red pepper"; adult comments on child's painting, "You painted a big cat," child says, "I made a little one, too").

Objective 5.2 Uses adjectives to make comparisons

CRITERION   Child uses adjectives to compare degrees of quality or quantity (e.g., child says, "My truck is best," "The red one is better," "She's the strongest one," "I have the most ice cream"; adult compares shapes child is using to make a collage by saying, "This circle is smaller than this one, and this circle is bigger," child says, "Here is the biggest one").

Objective 5.3 Uses adverbs

CRITERION   Child uses adverbs to modify verbs (e.g., child says, "That tastes bad," "Let's go fast," "He's talking loudly"; when child is pushing cars around race track, adult comments, "Look at those cars going around the track," child says, "They are going slow."

Objective 5.4 Uses prepositions

CRITERION   Child uses prepositions or prepositional phrases appropriately (e.g., child says, "Put it in the box," "It's on the table," "She's sitting beside him"; adult says, "The baseball bat is on the chair, but I don't see the ball," child says, "Let's look under the table"). The number of different prepositions used by the child is less important than the child's ability to use prepositions and prepositional phrases appropriate to the grammatical and semantic context of the sentence. Prepositions include the following:

up	off	like	in front of	near
for	over	at	in back of	on
down	of	by	through	under
in	with	to	out	

Objective 5.5 Uses conjunctions

CRITERION   Child uses conjunctions to connect words, phrases, and sentences (e.g., child says, "I want juice and a cookie," "We want to play, so we don't want to go to bed," "We could draw or color," "I like you because you're nice"; adult asks child to name all the foods child likes to eat, child says, "I like spaghetti and I like ice cream and pizza"). Conjunctions include the following:

| and | or | so | only |
| but | because | if | except |

Objective 5.6   Uses articles

CRITERION   Child uses articles (i.e., the, a, an) to precede nouns (e.g., "I want an ice cream cone," "I can't find the ball"; when selecting objects for water play, adult says, "I want the bucket, what do you want?", child says, "I want the sailboat").

AEPS™

Social Area
Three to Six Years

LIST OF AEPS TEST ITEMS

Social

NOTE

The development of social skills is closely related to and interdependent on the development of cognitive, communication, and adaptive skills; therefore, data from all areas should be considered by the AEPS Test user when reviewing Social Area items. The influence of cultural values on children's social behavior should also be considered during administration of the Social Area.

Social

Interaction with Others

GOAL 1   Interacts with others as play partners

CRITERION   Child interacts with others as play partners during daily activity by doing the following:

- Responding to others in distress or need

- Establishing and maintaining proximity to others

- Taking turns with others

- Initiating greeting to others who are familiar

- Responding to affective initiations from others

Interactions may be brief and the daily activities may be unstructured (e.g., child holds hand with peer and walks around the room singing a favorite song). Others may include peers, siblings, or familiar adults (e.g., family members, family friends, baby sitters).

NOTE   *If a child's performance on all objectives was scored with a 2, then the goal is scored 2. If a child's performance on the objectives was scored with any combination of a 0, 1, and 2, then the goal is scored 1. If a child's performance on all objectives was scored with a 0, then the goal is scored 0.*

Objective 1.1   Responds to others in distress or need

CRITERION   Child responds appropriately to others in distress or need (e.g., child pats peer who is crying; child helps peer move box of toys that is too heavy to move alone; child helps baby sitter clean up spilled juice).

Objective 1.2   Establishes and maintains proximity to others

CRITERION   Establishes and maintains proximity to others during unstructured, child-directed activity (e.g., child moves toward peer playing with blocks and plays with cars and a ramp next to peer; child moves toward peer playing in playhouse and plays with toys next to peer; child goes over to sandbox where older brother is playing and begins digging).

Objective 1.3   Takes turns with others

CRITERION   Child takes turns with others during daily activities (e.g., as timer sounds, child gets off bike and lets peer get on; child hands the watering can to a peer at the water table; child pushes sister on swing and then asks sister to give him a push; child waits with his or her hand raised while adult finishes story about a family trip.

Objective 1.4 **Initiates greetings to others who are familiar**

CRITERION   Child greets others with whom he or she is familiar by vocalizing, verbalizing, hugging, patting, touching, or smiling (e.g., child says, "Hi" to child care provider when he or she arrives in the morning; child squeals with pleasure when friend arrives at school; child runs and hugs dad when he sees him get out of his car).

Objective 1.5 **Responds to affective initiations from others**

CRITERION   Child demonstrates socially appropriate response to other's affective initiation (e.g., child smiles in response to peer's smile; child says, "Hi" in response to mom's greeting; child frowns and turns away in response to peer's anger; child hugs sister in response to sister snuggling close to the child).

GOAL 2   Initiates cooperative activity

CRITERION   Child uses verbal or nonverbal strategies to initiate cooperative activity and encourage peer(s) to participate. Cooperative activities are those that 1) require one or more peers; 2) encourage children to share/exchange or assist one another with materials; 3) contain jobs, roles, or identities for children to assume; and 4) often lead to mutual benefit for those participating (e.g., child says, "Come on, let's build a house" to group of peers; child assigns jobs, roles, or identities and encourages peers to carry them out; child says, "You play with this truck," while handing truck to peer as child pushes another truck; child says, "It's time to clean up" to group of peers, assigns jobs to be done, encourages peers to carry them out).

Objective 2.1 **Joins others in cooperative activity**

CRITERION   Child uses socially appropriate verbal or nonverbal strategies to join others engaged in cooperative activities (e.g., child approaches group of peers building a sand castle, sits next to them for a while, then begins to help peer who is digging a tunnel to the castle; child approaches peers playing house and

Social

says, "Hey, I could be the baby!", peer says, "Okay"; child approaches peers playing doctor and says, "Could I be the doctor?", peers say, "Well, okay").

Objective 2.2 Maintains cooperative participation with others

CRITERION   Child maintains job, role, or identity that supplements another child's job, role, or identity during a cooperative activity (e.g., peer says, "You hold these"; child holds two blocks together while peer puts a third block on top to build a house; child holds truck axle while peer puts a wheel on the axle).

Objective 2.3 Shares or exchanges objects

CRITERION   During daily activities, child shares or exchanges objects with other(s) engaged in the same activity (e.g., child shares glue bottle with peer when both are gluing leaves and flowers onto paper; child shares watercolor box with peer when both are painting pictures; child passes the juice to a peer at snack time; child trades puppets during circle time).

GOAL 3   Resolves conflicts by selecting effective strategy

CRITERION   Child selects appropriate strategies to resolve conflicts. Strategies include the following:

- Negotiating

- Using simple strategies

- Claiming and defending possessions

NOTE   *If a child's performance on all objectives was scored with a 2, then the goal is scored 2. If a child's performance on the objectives was scored with any combination of a 0, 1, and 2, then the goal is scored 1. If a child's performance on all objectives was scored with a 0, then the goal is scored 0.*

Objective 3.1 Negotiates to resolve conflicts

CRITERION   Child initiates a solution to bring about agreement when in conflict with a peer or adult (e.g., child says to a peer, "I'll dig here, and you dig there," when both want to dig in same corner of sandbox; child says to another child, "I'll play with the hammer, and you play with the saw," when both want to play with saw; child says, "I can play with it later," when asked by the teacher how to solve the problem of two children wanting to play with the same toy).

Objective 3.2   Uses simple strategies to resolve conflicts

CRITERION   Child uses variety of simple strategies (e.g., makes demands, walks/runs away, reports to adult) to resolve conflicts with another person (e.g., when peer hits child, child turns to adult and says, "Susan hit me"; child moves away from peer; when peer grabs toy from child, child says, "Give me").

Objective 3.3   Claims and defends possessions

CRITERION   Child uses verbal or nonverbal strategies to claim and defend possessions (e.g., child grabs back a toy from sister who has taken it; child says, "I had the block first," or "That toy is mine," takes toy from peer).

Participation

GOAL 1   Initiates and completes age-appropriate activities

CRITERION   Child initiates and completes age-appropriate activities without adult prompting (e.g., during free play, child gets out puzzle, puts it together, then puts it away; during free play, child goes to easel, paints picture, then hangs picture to dry).

Objective 1.1   Responds to request to finish activity

CRITERION   Child responds to first request to finish an activity (e.g., child carries out adult's request to pick up all of the blocks, to finish putting together a puzzle).

Objective 1.2   Responds to request to begin activity

CRITERION   Child responds to first request to begin an activity (e.g., child is sitting at table watching peers draw with crayons; child begins to draw with paper and crayons in response to adult's first request to do so).

GOAL 2   Watches, listens, and participates during small group activities

CRITERION   Child engages in the following behaviors during structured small group activities (i.e., group of five or fewer children):

- Interacts appropriately with materials

- Responds appropriately to directions

- Looks at appropriate object, person, or event

- Remains with group

Adult may provide group directions to help the child.

NOTE   *If a child's performance on all objectives was scored with a 2, then the goal is scored 2. If a child's performance on the objectives was scored with any combination of a 0, 1, and 2, then the goal is scored 1. If a child's performance on all objectives was scored with a 0, then the goal is scored 0.*

Objective 2.1   **Interacts appropriately with materials during small group activities**

CRITERION   Child interacts with materials in functional or demonstrated fashion during structured small group activities (i.e., group of five or fewer children). Adult may provide group directions.

Objective 2.2   **Responds appropriately to directions during small group activities**

CRITERION   Child responds with appropriate verbal or motor action to group directions provided by adult during structured small group activities (i.e., group of five or fewer children; e.g., during painting activity, child follows directions to dip paintbrush in paint and brush it across paper).

Objective 2.3   **Looks at appropriate object, person, or event during small group activities**

CRITERION   Child looks at object, person, or event that is focus of activity during structured small group activities (i.e., group of five or fewer children; e.g., child looks at adult while adult is talking; child looks at toy train that is topic of adult's conversation). Adult may provide group directions.

Objective 2.4   **Remains with group during small group activities**

CRITERION   Child stays in seat or in indicated area for duration of an activity during structured small group activities (i.e., group of five or fewer children; e.g., child remains in seat at table during table activity). Adult may provide group directions.

GOAL 3   **Watches, listens, and participates during large group activities**

CRITERION   Child engages in the following behaviors during large group activities (i.e., group of six or more children):

- Interacts appropriately with materials
- Responds appropriately to directions
- Looks at appropriate object, person, or event
- Remains with group

Adult may provide group directions to help the child.

Social

NOTE *If a child's performance on all objectives was scored with a 2, then the goal is scored 2. If a child's performance on the objectives was scored with any combination of a 0, 1, and 2, then the goal is scored 1. If a child's performance on all objectives was scored with a 0, then the goal is scored 0.*

Objective 3.1 Interacts appropriately with materials during large group activities

CRITERION Child interacts with materials in functional or demonstrated fashion during structured large group activities (i.e., group of six or more children; e.g., child passes ball to next child during group game). Adult may provide group directions.

Objective 3.2 Responds appropriately to directions during large group activities

CRITERION Child responds with appropriate verbal or motor action to group directions provided by adult during structured large group activities (i.e., group of six or more children; e.g., during music activity, child selects instrument, follows directions to play instrument).

Objective 3.3 Looks at appropriate object, person, or event during large group activities

CRITERION Child looks at object, person, or event that is focus of activity during structured large group activities (i.e., group of six or more children; e.g., during show-and-tell activity, child looks at person who is talking, showing toy boat). Adult may provide group directions.

Objective 3.4 Remains with group during large group activities

CRITERION Child stays in seat or indicated area for duration of an activity during large group activities (i.e., group of six or more children; e.g., child remains seated in place on floor or in chair during circle time; child remains in seat at table during snack time). Adult may provide group directions.

Interaction with Environment

GOAL 1   Meets physical needs in socially appropriate ways

CRITERION   Child uses socially appropriate strategies to meet physical needs such as the following:

- Physical needs when uncomfortable, sick, hurt, or tired

- Observable physical needs

- Physical needs of hunger and thirst

NOTE   *If a child's performance on all objectives was scored with a 2, then the goal is scored 2. If a child's performance on the objectives was scored with any combination of a 0, 1, and 2, then the goal is scored 1. If a child's performance on all objectives was scored with a 0, then the goal is scored 0.*

Objective 1.1   Meets physical needs when uncomfortable, sick, hurt, or tired

CRITERION: Child uses socially appropriate ways to meet physical needs when uncomfortable, sick, hurt, or tired (e.g., child requests adult help when injured or sick; child takes nap when tired; child puts on coat when cold; child lies down when not feeling well).

Objective 1.2   Meets observable physical needs

CRITERION   Child uses socially appropriate ways to meet observable physical needs (e.g., child washes hands when hands are dirty; child removes wet or soiled clothing).

Objective 1.3   Meets physical needs of hunger and thirst

CRITERION   Child uses socially appropriate ways to express or meet physical needs of hunger and thirst (e.g., child requests food, drink; child gets drink of milk when thirsty).

Social

GOAL 2   Follows context-specific rules outside home and classroom

CRITERION   Child follows context-specific rules outside home and classroom (e.g., store, park, doctor's office, restaurant, bus; child follows rule not to touch things when in grocery store; child follows rule to remain in seat during bus ride; during a walk, child holds a peer's hand in response to adult's directions). This item should be scored with parent input to determine how the child follows rules outside of the classroom.

Objective 2.1   Seeks adult permission

CRITERION   Child asks adult permission in order to engage in established routines at home, at school, and in the community (e.g., child asks permission to leave the group, go to the bathroom; child asks caregiver for permission to go to neighbor's house; child asks permission to take out the playdough after finishing a group activity). This item should be scored with parent input to determine how the child follows rules outside of the classroom.

Objective 2.2   Follows established rules at home and in classroom

CRITERION   Child follows established rules at home and in the classroom (e.g., child washes hands before snack time, waits turn to speak; during large group activity, child raises hand to be recognized; child does not run in house). Adult may provide group directions/cues (e.g., "It's story time," "Time to line up"). This item should be scored with parent input to determine how child follows rules outside the classroom.

Knowledge of Self and Others

GOAL 1   Communicates personal likes and dislikes

CRITERION   Child uses verbal and/or nonverbal strategies to communicate personal likes and dislikes, including

- Initiating preferred activities (e.g., child will select puzzle from choice of toys)

- Selecting activities or objects (e.g., child says, "I like cake better than apples," "I don't want to play outside today")

NOTE   *If a child's performance on all objectives was scored with a 2, then the goal is scored 2. If a child's performance on the objectives was scored with any combination of a 0, 1, and 2, then the goal is scored 1. If a child's performance on all objectives was scored with a 0, then the goal is scored 0.*

Objective 1.1   Initiates preferred activities

CRITERION   Child initiates preferred purposeful activities during free time (e.g., child goes to shelf, selects book to look at during play; child finishes work, gets paper and markers for coloring; child chooses to play with blocks with a peer). General cues may be provided by adult (e.g., "Find something to do").

Objective 1.2   Selects activities and/or objects

CRITERION   Child selects an activity or object when given a choice (e.g., child selects crackers from a plate of crackers and cheese; child selects puzzle from a table with books, puzzles, tea set; child chooses to paint from a choice of three activities; child selects an apple from a basket of apples, bananas, oranges).

GOAL 2   Understands how own behaviors, thoughts, and feelings relate to consequences for others

CRITERION   Child demonstrates understanding of how own behaviors, thoughts, and feelings relate to consequences for others (e.g., after grabbing peer's favorite toy, returns toy as peer starts to cry; after noticing that peer did not get a cracker, child passes plate back to peer; child tells sibling as they both run to the car, "You can have the window seat"; child selects peer who is often chosen last as a teammate).

Objective 2.1   Identifies affect/emotions of others

CRITERION   Child identifies affect/emotions of others that are consistent with behaviors being displayed (e.g., child signs, "He's hurt," in response to a peer's crying after falling on the playground; child says, "She likes it," in response to a peer smiling at getting a favorite cookie during snack time).

Objective 2.2   Identifies own affect/emotions

CRITERION   Child identifies own affect/emotions that are consistent with displayed behaviors (e.g., child frowns and says, "Yuck, I don't like it," after sampling distasteful food; child cries after losing a doll and says, "I'm sad"; child throws toy and stomps away from play area, teacher asks, "What happened?", child says, "I'm mad").

GOAL 3   Relates identifying information about self and others

CRITERION   Child correctly communicates the following information about self and others:

- Address (number, street, and town)

- Telephone number

- Birthday (month and day)

- Names of siblings and full name of self

- Gender (self and others)

- First name and age

NOTE   *If a child's performance on all objectives was scored with a 2, then the goal is scored 2. If a child's performance on the objectives was scored with any combination of a 0, 1, and 2, then the goal is scored 1. If a child's performance on all objectives was scored with a 0, then the goal is scored 0.*

Objective 3.1   States address

CRITERION   Child correctly states own address (including number, street, and town).

Objective 3.2   States telephone numbers

CRITERION   Child correctly states at least two telephone numbers (e.g., child recites own telephone number, parents work number, an emergency number, grandma's house).

Objective 3.3   States birthday

CRITERION   Child correctly states month and day of own birthday.

Objective 3.4   Names siblings and gives full name of self

CRITERION   Child correctly states first names of siblings and first and last names of self.

Objective 3.5   States gender of self and others

CRITERION   Child correctly identifies self and others as a girl or a boy.

Objective 3.6   States name and age

CRITERION   Child correctly states own first name and age in years.

APPENDIX

A

AEPS Assessment Activities

Birth to Three Years

Three to Six Years

As discussed in Chapter 4 of this volume, beginning users of the AEPS Test are advised to start with assessment that is focused on a single area with one child. As users become familiar with the AEPS Test, they can learn to assess two or more children across developmental areas. There are clear limits to the number of children and areas that can be assessed simultaneously; however, being able to assess several children at the same time reaps important time savings as does assessing children across developmental areas. To assist AEPS Test users to either assess more than one child or to assess children across areas, assessment activities are contained in this appendix.

The use of assessment activities should contribute to two important outcomes. First, use of the assessment activities should help interventionists obtain an accurate picture of a child's functional repertoire (e.g., what skills he or she has and how these skills are used). Second, the use of the assessment activities should result in economies that may permit beginning intervention efforts more quickly.

The assessment activities contained in this appendix can serve two distinct purposes. First, they can be used as they are written to assess a variety of children across developmental areas. Second, they can serve as models for the development of alternative assessment activities that might better meet the needs of particular children, interventionists, and programs.

Each of the 12 assessment activities presented in this appendix contains the following information:

- The name of the assessment activity (e.g., Story)

- The target developmental level (i.e., birth to three years or three to six years)

- Potential areas the assessment activity can address (e.g., Social)

- Materials needed

- A running description of the activity

- A list of goals or objectives by area and strand

- Space for recording performance data (i.e., S column for score and N column for scoring notes) for up to four children

Each of the 12 assessment activities is organized in sequential order. That is, the activity is described in sequential segments beginning with the initiation of the activity and what might be logical steps during the activity to its completion. For each segment of the activity, goals/objectives that are likely to be observed are listed. Table 9 lists the assessment activities for both levels of the AEPS.

Table 9. Assessment Activities

Birth to Three Years	Three to Six Years
Books and Formboards	Activity Centers/
Circle Games	Free Play
Dolls	Obstacle Course
Magic Show	Playdough
Roads and Bridges	Post Office
Snack	Story
Water Play	

HOW TO USE THE ASSESSMENT ACTIVITIES

To begin, interventionists will want to study the 12 assessment activities provided in order to select those that may potentially address a child's or children's areas of concern. Each assessment activity should be studied to ensure that critical goals and objectives will be assessed. Interventionists should also consider the inherent interest of the activity for their children.

Once assessment activities are selected, the interventionists will need to identify which child or children could or should participate. There should be a match between children's areas of development that need assessing and the potential goals/objectives targeted by the assessment activity. Interventionists may find that all or most of the assessment activities described in this appendix will require moderate to significant modification to make them appropriate for their children and their circumstances.

After assessment activities are selected for a child or group of children, interventionists may find it useful to organize a series of assessment stations as shown in Figure 4. A different activity can be conducted at each station, and small groups of children can move from station to station.

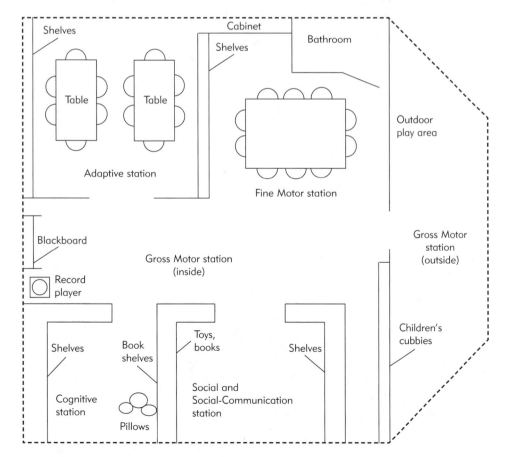

Figure 4. An example of a center-based program arranged in stations for conducting assessment.

Whether interventionists choose to use a series of stations or organize the assessment activities in some other way, preplanning is essential. First, the location for the assessment activities should be considered. Options can range from a specific location in the room or outdoors to a more general free play arrangement that may overlap several areas in a room. Once a location is determined, interventionists need to give consideration to how the area might be arranged, whether additional equipment is needed, and what materials should be available to the children; for example, if the Post Office Assessment Activity is to be used, it may be useful to have or create a counter (e.g., a table could be used) and a mailbox; paper, writing/cutting implements, and stamp-making materials should be available. For the Dolls Assessment Activity, an area close to water and easy to clean up is advisable. Small tubs or containers, dolls, clothing, towels, sponges, and so forth should be accessible to the children.

HOW TO SCORE ASSESSMENT ACTIVITIES

As children engage in the activity segments, the AEPS Test user can observe their activities and score their performance on the listed goals/objectives. Criteria for the items are contained in Sections II and III of this volume. The three-point scoring option (2, 1, or 0) should be employed. Scoring notes can also be used.

BOOKS AND FORMBOARDS

Developmental level: Birth to Three Years

Potential assessment areas: Fine Motor, Cognitive, Social-Communication, Social

Materials: Formboard with simple geometric shapes; picture books that contain clear pictures of common animals and objects; toy animals that match the pictures; picture books with common signs, symbols, logos; book of nursery rhymes

STEP 1

Group two to three children at a table or on the floor in an area where other materials have been removed. Introduce formboards with simple geometric shapes. Allow each child opportunities to put the shapes into the corresponding spaces on the formboard. Remove formboards and introduce picture books containing pictures of animals and objects that are familiar to the children. Present books upside down, and observe if each child orients book correctly. Observe if each child is able to turn pages one at a time. As children interact with books, observe whether they make comments and ask questions while looking at books. Encourage children to locate common animals in the book by commenting about them, pausing to allow the children to point to them, or to point to and label other objects in the book. Observe each child's ability to locate common animals and objects in the pictures with and without contextual cues.

Area and strand		Goals/objectives	Children's initials							
			S	N	S	N	S	N	S	N
FM B	2.1	Fits variety of shapes into corresponding spaces								
	G4	Orients picture book correctly and turns pages one by one								
Cog G	4.2	Makes comments and asks questions while looking at picture books								
SC C	G1	Locates objects, people, and/or events without contextual cues								
	1.1	Locates common objects, people, and/or events in unfamiliar pictures								
	1.3	Locates common objects, people, and/or events with contextual cues								

STEP 2

Arrange the toy animals so that they are visible and accessible to the children. Point to a picture of an animal in one of the children's books and encourage the child to find the toy animal that matches. Observe each child's ability to point to matching pictures and objects. Engage in parallel play, and model pretend events with the toy animals; for example, pretend the animals have proper names and roles and are engaged in some activities that are familiar to the child but unlikely to occur to animals, such as making the cows talk on the phone or drive a tractor. Allow the children to direct the play sequence after your initial modeling. Observe each child's ability to use representational actions with objects and to use imaginary objects in play.

			|	Children's initials							
Area and strand		**Goals/objectives**									
			S	**N**	**S**	**N**	**S**	**N**	**S**	**N**
Cog F	G1	Uses imaginary objects in play								
	1.1	Uses representational actions with objects								
Cog G	1.3	Matches pictures and/or objects								

STEP 3

Remove animal picture books and introduce books with common signs and symbols such as "Stop," men's and women's restroom symbols, and "Exit." Ask children to identify symbols when asked. Introduce a storybook with familiar nursery rhymes, and announce that you will read to them. Observe children's ability to attend to the nursery rhyme. As you read, ask children to say the rhyme along with you. While reading another rhyme, stop before the end and observe child's ability to fill in missing words to a familiar rhyme. Ask children if they know a familiar nursery rhyme such as Pat-a-Cake or Itsy Bitsy Spider. Observe each child's social and communicative interactions with adults and peers.

			|	Children's initials							
Area and strand		**Goals/objectives**									
			S	**N**	**S**	**N**	**S**	**N**	**S**	**N**
Cog G	G3	Recognizes environmental symbols (signs, logos, labels)								
	4.3	Sits and attends to entire story during shared reading time								
	G6	Repeats simple nursery rhymes								
	6.1	Fills in rhyming words in familiar rhymes								

Area and strand		Goals/objectives	Children's initials							
			S	N	S	N	S	N	S	N
Cog G	6.2	Says nursery rhymes along with familiar adult								
Soc A	G2	Initiates and maintains interaction with familiar adult								
	G3	Initiates and maintains communicative exchange with familiar adult								
Soc C	G1	Initiates and maintains interaction with peer								
	G2	Initiates and maintains communicative exchange with peer								

CIRCLE GAMES

Developmental level: Birth to Three Years

Potential assessment areas: Gross Motor, Cognitive

Materials: Balls; tub or other container; rope or tape to make a line; foam rubber blocks

STEP 1

Group two to three children in a semi-circle on the floor. Observe each child's ability to sit and recover sitting position throughout the activity. Place the balls in a low container about 5 feet from the children, and place a rope or line midway between the children and the container of balls. Encourage each child, in turn, to get up and jump over the line and obtain a ball. Observe each child's ability to stoop and resume a standing position without support. Observe each child's ability to jump forward. Gather all the balls and resume sitting on the floor in a circle. Begin a rolling game with one ball. Observe each child's ability to roll a ball toward another person. Observe children's ability to repeat actions in order to continue the activity.

		Goals/objectives	Children's initials							
Area and strand			S	N	S	N	S	N	S	N
GM B	G1	Assumes balanced sitting position								
	1.1	Assumes hands and knees position from sitting								
	1.2	Regains balanced, upright sitting position after reaching across the body to the right and to the left								
	1.3	Regains balanced, upright sitting position after leaning to the left, to the right, and forward								
	1.4	Sits balanced without support								
	1.5	Sits balanced using hands for support								
	1.6	Holds head in midline when in supported sitting position								
GM C	G2	Stoops and regains balanced standing position without support								
	2.1	Rises from sitting position to standing position								

Area and strand		Goals/objectives	Children's initials							
			S	N	S	N	S	N	S	N
GM C	2.2	Pulls to standing position								
	2.3	Pulls to kneeling position								
GM D	G1	Jumps forward								
	3.4	Rolls ball at target								
Cog C	G2	Reproduces part of interactive game and/or action in order to continue game and/or action								
	2.1	Indicates desire to continue familiar game and/or action								

STEP 2

Encourage children to throw a ball toward another person and catch a ball that has been gently tossed to them. After each child has had multiple opportunities to demonstrate rolling, throwing, and catching skills, allow each child several opportunities to kick a ball toward a tub or other container.

Area and strand		Goals/objectives	Children's initials							
			S	N	S	N	S	N	S	N
GM D	3.1	Catches ball or similar object								
	3.2	Kicks ball or similar object								
	3.3	Throws ball or similar object at target								

STEP 3

Randomly place several foam rubber blocks (or other forgiving objects) on the floor as obstacles for the children. While the children are throwing and retrieving balls, observe each child's ability to walk avoiding obstacles, to walk without support, to walk with one- or two-hand support, and/or to cruise. Observe each child's ability to run avoiding obstacles and to run and/or walk fast.

Area and strand		Goals/objectives	Children's initials							
			S	N	S	N	S	N	S	N
GM C	G1	Walks avoiding obstacles								

Area and strand		Goals/objectives	Children's initials							
			S	N	S	N	S	N	S	N
GM C	1.1	Walks without support								
	1.2	Walks with one-hand support								
	1.3	Walks with two-hand support								
	1.4	Stands unsupported								
	1.5	Cruises								
	G3	Runs avoiding obstacles								
	3.1	Runs								
	3.2	Walks fast								

DOLLS

Developmental level: Birth to Three Years

Potential assessment areas: Gross Motor, Cognitive, Social

Materials: Dolls; bathing and grooming items (e.g., soap, washcloths, comb, brush); clothes for dressing dolls; food and dishes for feeding dolls (e.g., cups, bottles, plates, spoons); containers that are labeled with pictures (e.g., a container for food that has pictures of dairy products, fruits, meats; a container for doll clothes that has pictures of dresses, pants, shoes)

STEP 1

Group two to three children at a child-size table in an area where all other toys have been removed. Observe each child's ability to get into and out of a child-size chair. Give a doll to each child to play with while you arrange other materials so that they are visible and accessible to the children (e.g., bathing and grooming items, clothes, food, dishes). From a group of items (e.g., washcloths, bottles, combs) ask one child to give one item to each of the other children. Give children suggestions about what they can do with their dolls such as, "Can you give your baby a bath?" or "Your baby is hungry, she needs some food." Observe each child's ability to gather several items appropriate for feeding, bathing, or dressing. Observe how the children interact with the dolls. Are they pretending to feed, bathe, and/or rock the baby to sleep? Do they use objects to represent other objects as they pretend (e.g., a child uses a block to call the doctor because his or her baby is sick)?

Area and strand		Goals/objectives	Children's initials							
			S	N	S	N	S	N	S	N
GM B	G2	Sits down in and gets out of chair								
	2.1	Sits down in chair								
	2.2	Maintains a sitting position in chair								
Cog G	1.1	Groups functionally related objects								
	G2	Demonstrates functional use of one-to-one correspondence								
	2.1	Demonstrates concept of one								

Area and strand		Goals/objectives	Children's initials							
			S	N	S	N	S	N	S	N
Cog F	G1	Uses imaginary objects in play								
	1.1	Uses representational actions with objects								
	1.2	Uses functionally appropriate actions with objects								
	1.3	Uses simple motor actions on different objects								
	1.4	Uses sensory examination with objects								

STEP 2 Provide the children opportunities to play with the toys without direction. If necessary, encourage interactive play and communication by demonstrating parallel play interspersed with occasional verbal and gestural interactions with the children. Follow the lead of the children by decreasing your actions and interactions as the children's physical and verbal interactions increase. Observe each child's social and communicative interactions with both adults and peers.

Area and strand		Goals/objectives	Children's initials							
			S	N	S	N	S	N	S	N
Soc A	G2	Initiates and maintains interaction with familiar adult								
	2.1	Initiates simple social game with familiar adult								
	2.2	Responds to familiar adult's social behavior								
	G3	Initiates and maintains communicative exchange with familiar adult								
	3.1	Initiates communication with familiar adult								
	3.2	Responds to communication from familiar adult								

Area and strand		Goals/objectives	Children's initials							
			S	N	S	N	S	N	S	N
Soc C	G1	Initiates and maintains interaction with peer								
	1.1	Initiates social behavior toward peer								
	1.2	Responds appropriately to peer's social behavior								
	1.3	Plays near one or two peers								
	1.4	Observes peers								
	1.5	Entertains self by playing appropriately with toys								
	G2	Initiates and maintains communicative exchange with peer								
	2.1	Initiates communication with peer								
	2.2	Responds to communication from peer								

STEP 3 When it is time to end the activity, bring out containers for sorting. Show the children the pictures on each container and say, "Let's put all of the food in this container." Present different items to the children, and observe each child's ability to group similar objects (e.g., all clothing items in one container, all dishes in a different container, all food items in another container).

Area and strand		Goals/objectives	Children's initials							
			S	N	S	N	S	N	S	N
Cog G	G1	Categorizes like objects								
	1.1	Groups functionally related objects								
	1.3	Matches pictures and/or objects								

Developmental level: Birth to Three Years

Potential assessment areas: Fine Motor, Cognitive, Social-Communication

Materials: Paper; markers with lids; box or other container; small objects (e.g., pennies, toy animals, stickers)

Group two to three children at a table in an area where all other materials have been removed. Introduce one piece of paper to each child, telling all the children that after they do something special with the paper, it will be used for magic. Allow each child to choose one marker. Draw written shapes (e.g., cross, square, circle, line) on the paper one at a time, allowing the children an opportunity to duplicate each figure you have drawn in turn. Then allow the children to draw independently. Observe their ability to scribble and/or copy simple shapes after demonstration. After all of the children have had an opportunity to draw, ask each child to fit the top back on the marker before putting it away, and observe their ability to assemble the two parts of the marker.

Area and strand		Goals/objectives	Children's initials							
			S	N	S	N	S	N	S	N
FM B	G2	Assembles toy and/or object that require(s) putting pieces together								
	G5	Copies simple written shapes after demonstration								
	5.1	Draws circles and lines								
	5.2	Scribbles								

Tell the children that you are going to do some magic now. Take the three pieces of paper from the children and arrange them on the table. Using the paper as a cover, first hide a small object under one piece of paper, then move it under a second piece of paper. Observe each child's ability, in turn, to locate the object in the latter of two successive hiding places and/or visually follow the object to the point of disappearance. If children have difficulty finding the hidden object, then try hiding the object so that it is partially in view, or hide the object under the table, under the paper, or behind your back while the children are watching.

Area and strand		Goals/objectives	Children's initials							
			S	N	S	N	S	N	S	N
Cog B	G1	Visually follows object and/or person to point of disappearance								
	1.2	Focuses on object and/or person								
	G2	Locates object in latter of two successive hiding places								
	2.1	Locates object and/or person hidden while child is watching								
	2.2	Locates object and/or person who is partially hidden while child is watching								
	2.3	Reacts when object and/or person hides from view								

STEP 3

Continue hiding objects and give each child opportunities to repeat a "magic word" and a "magic action" prior to lifting the paper to locate the object. The magic word should be one that is not frequently used by the child, but it should contain developmentally appropriate sounds and it should be easy for the child to say. Observe each child's ability to imitate the word. If a child cannot imitate words, then model "magic sounds" that are not frequently used by the child but that contain developmentally appropriate consonant–vowel combinations. Words that are frequently used by the child may also be modeled. Observe the child's ability to imitate the sounds. Model motor actions both familiar to the children (e.g., clapping) and novel (e.g., moving your hand in a circular motion over the paper or box). Encourage children to imitate before allowing them opportunities to locate hidden objects. Observe each child's ability to imitate motor actions that are both commonly used and not commonly used.

Area and strand		Goals/objectives	Children's initials							
			S	N	S	N	S	N	S	N
Cog D	G2	Imitates words that are not frequently used								
	2.1	Imitates speech sounds that are not frequently used								

Area and strand		Goals/objectives	Children's initials							
			S	N	S	N	S	N	S	N
Cog D	2.2	Imitates words that are frequently used								
	G1	Imitates motor action that is not commonly used								
	1.1	Imitates motor action that is commonly used								

STEP 4

Encourage children to follow one- and two-step directions that do not relate to the immediate context before locating hidden objects (e.g., tell a child to "Touch your nose, then clap your hands"; "Touch your shoulder"). Observe each child's ability to carry out directions without contextual cues.

Area and strand		Goals/objectives	Children's initials							
			S	N	S	N	S	N	S	N
SC C	G2	Carries out two-step direction without contextual cues								
	2.2	Carries out one-step direction without contextual cues								

ROADS AND BRIDGES

Developmental level: Birth to Three Years

Potential assessment areas: Fine Motor, Gross Motor, Cognitive, Social

Materials: Blocks of assorted shapes, sizes, colors; containers with snap-on lids; variety of small cars, trucks, airplanes, and other vehicles with toy people and animals; small mechanical toys

STEP 1

Group two to three children on the floor in an area where all other materials have been removed. Introduce a closed container of blocks to each child in turn. Observe the strategies each child employs while attempting to open the container. Help the children open containers if they request help.

Area and strand		Goals/objectives	Children's initials							
			S	N	S	N	S	N	S	N
Cog E	G4	Solves common problems								
	4.1	Uses more than one strategy in attempt to solve common problem								

STEP 2

Allow children to explore blocks independently for several minutes. Observe each child's ability to reach for and grasp hand-size objects. Note the type of grasp that the child exhibits and how he or she is able to manipulate objects as you score the goals and objectives listed. If children do not demonstrate those skills, then engage in parallel play beside the children by building roads, towers, and bridges, and/or aligning blocks to make a "train."

Area and strand		Goals/objectives	Children's initials							
			S	N	S	N	S	N	S	N
FM A	G2	Brings two objects together at or near midline								
	2.1	Transfers object from one hand to the other								
	2.2	Holds an object in each hand								
	2.3	Reaches toward and touches object with each hand								

Area and strand		Goals/objectives	Children's initials							
			S	N	S	N	S	N	S	N
FM A	G3	Grasps hand-size object with either hand using ends of thumb, index, and second fingers								
	G5	Aligns and stacks objects								
Cog E	G1	Retains objects when new object is obtained								
	1.1	Retains one object when second object is obtained								

STEP 3

Introduce toy vehicles, airplanes, and people. Observe each child's ability to fit people into vehicles and vehicles under block bridges. Make the toy airplanes "fly," and observe each child's ability to visually follow the plane in horizontal, vertical, and circular directions. Make the airplane "disappear," and observe child's ability to follow it to the point of disappearance.

Area and strand		Goals/objectives	Children's initials							
			S	N	S	N	S	N	S	N
FM B	2.1	Fits variety of shapes into corresponding spaces								
	2.2	Fits object into defined space								
Cog B	G1	Visually follows object and/or person to point of disappearance								
	1.1	Visually follows object moving in horizontal, vertical, and circular directions								

STEP 4

Introduce mechanical vehicles that must be activated to produce an action. Observe each child's ability to correctly activate mechanical toys. If the toys are novel to the children, then activate them so that each child is aware of the action produced by the toy. Observe each child's ability to activate the toy with the index finger, if appropriate, or with horizontal wrist rotation.

Area and strand		Goals/objectives	Children's initials							
			S	N	S	N	S	N	S	N
Cog C	G1	Correctly activates mechanical toy								
	G2	Reproduces part of interactive game and/or action in order to continue game and/or action								
FM B	G1	Rotates either wrist on horizontal plane								
	G3	Uses either index finger to activate objects								

STEP 5

To clean up the activity, remove all vehicles and people but do not remove the wood blocks. Provide containers and sort several blocks into each container according to some characteristic of the block (e.g., color, size). Request help in cleaning up by handing a block to each child in turn and asking, "Where does this go?" Observe each child's ability to sort according to size, shape, or color. Observe each child's ability to release a hand-held object with each hand and to release an object into the container with either hand.

Area and strand		Goals/objectives	Children's initials							
			S	N	S	N	S	N	S	N
Cog G	1.2	Groups objects according to size, shape, and/or color								
FM A	5.3	Releases hand-held object onto and/or into a larger target with either hand								
	5.4	Releases hand-held object with each hand								

STEP 6

Throughout the activity, provide children opportunities to move and interact with people and materials freely. Observe each child's ability to sit balanced without support, to sit balanced using hands for support, and/or to hold head in midline when in a supported position. Observe each child's ability to assume a balanced sitting position; to assume hands and knees position from sitting; to regain a balanced sitting position after reaching across the body to the left and the right; and to regain a balanced sitting position after leaning to the left, right, and forward.

Area and strand		Goals/objectives	Children's initials							
			S	N	S	N	S	N	S	N
GM B	G1	Assumes balanced sitting position								
	1.1	Assumes hands and knees position from sitting								
	1.2	Regains balanced, upright sitting position after reaching across the body to the right and to the left								
	1.3	Regains balanced, upright sitting position after leaning to the left, to the right, and forward								
	1.4	Sits balanced without support								
	1.5	Sits balanced using hands for support								
	1.6	Holds head in midline when in supported sitting position								

SNACK

Developmental level: Birth to Three Years

Potential assessment areas: Adaptive, Fine Motor, Gross Motor, Cognitive

Materials: Child-size cups, small bowls, napkins, spoons; juice in light-weight pitchers; raisins in small transparent jar with twist-off lid; yogurt or applesauce; foods in pieces large enough to require the children to bite (e.g., quartered apples, saltine crackers); waterproof tarp to protect floor; bibs or child-size aprons

STEP 1

Place a child-size table on a tarp without chairs around it, in a semi-enclosed area. Request that two to four children retrieve a chair and bring it to the table to get ready for snack. Observe each child's ability to navigate the chair (i.e., large object) around barriers in the room (including the table), move barriers or go around barriers to obtain chairs, and move around barriers to change location.

Area and strand		Goals/objectives	Children's initials							
			S	N	S	N	S	N	S	N
Cog E	G3	Navigates large object around barriers								
	3.1	Moves barrier or goes around barrier to obtain object								
	3.2	Moves around barrier to change location								

STEP 2

Group children at the table. Observe each child's ability to get into and out of a child-size chair. Allow children to distribute the eating utensils (e.g., bowls, cups, spoons, napkins). Observe each child's ability to assign one object to two or more people. (If a child does not successfully assign one item to two or more people, then allow the child additional opportunities.)

Area and strand		Goals/objectives	Children's initials							
			S	N	S	N	S	N	S	N
GM B	G2	Sits down in and gets out of chair								
	2.1	Sits down in chair								

Area and strand		Goals/objectives	Children's initials							
			S	N	S	N	S	N	S	N
GM B	2.2	Maintains a sitting position in chair								
Cog G	G2	Demonstrates functional use of one-to-one correspondence								
	2.1	Demonstrates concept of one								

STEP 3

Offer raisins in a small, transparent jar to children. The lid on the jar should require the child to unscrew it, but it should not be secured too tightly. Observe each child's ability to rotate wrist on a horizontal plane while opening the jar. Allow each child to put the lid back on the jar before passing it on to the next child. Observe each child's ability to assemble the jar and lid. If the child cannot open or close the jar successfully, then observe the child's use of alternative strategies to solve problems. Observe each child's grasp when obtaining raisins and other small pieces of food and when grasping a spoon.

Area and strand		Goals/objectives	Children's initials							
			S	N	S	N	S	N	S	N
FM B	G1	Rotates either wrist on horizontal plane								
	1.1	Turns object over using wrist and arm rotation with each hand								
	G2	Assembles toy and/or object that require(s) putting pieces together								
	2.1	Fits variety of shapes into corresponding spaces								
	2.2	Fits object into defined space								
Cog E	G4	Solves common problems								
	4.1	Uses more than one strategy in attempt to solve common problem								
FM A	G3	Grasps hand-size object with either hand using ends of thumb, index, and second fingers								

Area and strand		Goals/objectives	Children's initials							
			S	N	S	N	S	N	S	N
FM A	3.1	Grasps hand-size object with either hand using the palm, with object placed toward the thumb and index finger								
	3.2	Grasps cylindrical object with either hand by closing fingers around it								
	3.3	Grasps hand-size object with either hand using whole hand								
	G4	Grasps pea-size object with either hand using tip of the index finger and thumb with hand and/or arm not resting on surface for support								
	4.1	Grasps pea-size object with either hand using tip of the index finger and thumb with hand and/or arm resting on surface for support								
	4.2	Grasps pea-size object with either hand using side of the index finger and thumb								
	4.3	Grasps pea-size object with either hand using fingers in a raking and/or scratching movement								

STEP 4 *Allow children opportunities to pour juice into their own cups. Observe each child's ability to transfer liquids. Allow children opportunities to spoon yogurt or applesauce into their own bowls. Observe each child's ability to transfer food with a spoon. Observe each child's ability to eat a variety of foods, to eat independently with a spoon or fork, and to drink from a cup.*

Area and strand		Goals/objectives	Children's initials							
			S	N	S	N	S	N	S	N
Adap A	G1	Uses tongue and lips to take in and swallow solid foods and liquids								

Area and strand		Goals/objectives	Children's initials							
			S	N	S	N	S	N	S	N
Adap A	1.1	Uses lips to take in liquids from a cup and/or glass								
	1.2	Uses lips to take food off spoon and/or fork								
	1.3	Swallows solid and semi-solid foods								
	1.4	Swallows liquids								
	G2	Bites and chews hard and chewy foods								
	2.1	Bites and chews soft and crisp foods								
	2.2	Munches soft and crisp foods								
	G3	Drinks from cup and/or glass								
	3.1	Drinks from cup and/or glass with some spilling								
	3.2	Drinks from cup and/or glass held by adult								
	G4	Eats with fork and/or spoon								
	4.1	Brings food to mouth using utensil								
	4.2	Eats with fingers								
	G5	Transfers food and liquid between containers								
	5.1	Pours liquid between containers								
	5.2	Transfers food between containers								

WATER PLAY

Developmental level: Birth to Three Years

Potential assessment areas: Social, Social-Communication, Gross Motor, Cognitive

Materials: Aprons or bibs to protect children's clothing; container for water (e.g., large tubs, water table, small wading pool); variety of toys for water play (e.g., toy boats with strings attached for pulling, toy people to fit inside, toy animals); waterproof mechanical toys (i.e., require activation); waterproof tarp to protect floor

STEP 1

Group two to three children at a child-size table in an area that is protected with a waterproof tarp. Observe each child's ability to sit in and get out of a child-size chair. Introduce the boats by placing them on a deep shelf or cupboard at child's eye level but out of the child's reach; the attached string should be within the child's reach. Observe each child's ability to obtain a boat by pulling on the attached string or using an alternative strategy (e.g., climbing on a chair, asking an adult).

Area and strand		Goals/objectives	Children's initials							
			S	N	S	N	S	N	S	N
GM B	G2	Sits down in and gets out of chair								
	2.1	Sits down in chair								
	2.2	Maintains a sitting position in chair								
Cog E	G2	Uses an object to obtain another object								
	2.1	Uses part of object and/or support to obtain another object								
	G4	Solves common problems								
	4.1	Uses more than one strategy in attempt to solve common problem								

STEP 2

Record a separate sample of verbatim language for each child as the children interact. As you review each sample following the activity, note the grammatical forms used by each child.

Area and strand	Goals/objectives	Children's initials							
		S	N	S	N	S	N	S	N
SC D	G1, G2, and G3 can be assessed with a language sample and transferred to an AEPS protocol								

STEP 3

Introduce all toys except the mechanical ones. Encourage interactive play and communication by demonstrating parallel play interspersed with occasional verbal and gestural interactions with the children (e.g., interventionist makes toy person talk, "Oh, I'm jumping into the boat. Uh oh, I fell! Now I have to swim to the boat"). Simultaneously make your toys act out the scene you are describing. Allow the children opportunities to talk and play by pausing in your play. Follow the children's lead by decreasing your actions and interactions as their physical and verbal interactions increase. Observe each child's play behavior, and note functional and representational play. Observe each child's social and communicative interactions with both adults and peers. Throughout the activity, observe each child's ability to use social-communicative interactions.

Area and strand		Goals/objectives	Children's initials							
			S	N	S	N	S	N	S	N
Soc A	G1	Responds appropriately to familiar adult's affect								
	1.1	Displays affection toward familiar adult								
	1.2	Responds appropriately to familiar adult's affective tone								
	1.3	Smiles in response to familiar adult								
	G2	Initiates and maintains interaction with familiar adult								
	2.1	Initiates simple social game with familiar adult								
	2.2	Responds to familiar adult's social behavior								

Area and strand		Goals/objectives	Children's initials							
			S	N	S	N	S	N	S	N
Soc A	2.3	Uses familiar adults for comfort, closeness, or physical contact								
	G3	Initiates and maintains communicative exchange with familiar adult								
	3.1	Initiates communication with familiar adult								
	3.2	Responds to communication from familiar adult								
Cog F	G1	Uses imaginary objects in play								
	1.1	Uses representational actions with objects								
	1.2	Uses functionally appropriate actions with objects								
	1.3	Uses simple motor actions on different objects								
	1.4	Uses sensory examination with objects								
Soc C	G1	Initiates and maintains interaction with peer								
	1.1	Initiates social behavior toward peer								
	1.2	Responds appropriately to peer's social behavior								
	1.3	Plays near one or two peers								
	1.4	Observes peers								
	1.5	Entertains self by playing appropriately with toys								
	G2	Initiates and maintains communicative exchange with peer								
	2.1	Initiates communication with peer								
	2.2	Responds to communication from peer								

Area and strand		Goals/objectives	Children's initials							
			S	N	S	N	S	N	S	N
SC A	G1	Turns and looks toward person speaking								
	1.1	Turns and looks toward object and person speaking								
	1.2	Turns and looks toward noise-producing object								
	G2	Follows person's gaze to establish joint attention								
	2.1	Follows person's pointing gesture to establish joint attention								
	2.2	Looks toward an object								
	G3	Engages in vocal exchanges by babbling								
	3.1	Engages in vocal exchanges by cooing								

STEP 4 — *Present one- and two-step verbal directions and observe each child's ability to follow your directions when you provide cues as well as when there are no cues provided. Introduce mechanical toys that must be activated to produce an action. Observe each child's ability to correctly activate the mechanical toys. If the toys are novel to the children, activate them so that the children are aware of the action produced by the toy.*

Area and strand		Goals/objectives	Children's initials							
			S	N	S	N	S	N	S	N
SC C	G1	Locates objects, people, and/or events without contextual cues								
	1.3	Locates common objects, people, and/or events with contextual cues								
	G2	Carries out two-step direction without contextual cues								
	2.1	Carries out two-step direction with contextual cues								

Area and strand		Goals/objectives	Children's initials							
			S	N	S	N	S	N	S	N
SC C	2.2	Carries out one-step direction without contextual cues								
	2.3	Carries out one-step direction with contextual cues								
Cog C	G1	Correctly activates mechanical toy								
	1.1	Correctly activates simple toy								
	1.2	Acts on mechanical and/or simple toy in some way								
	1.3	Indicates interest in simple and/or mechanical toy								
	G2	Reproduces part of interactive game and/or action in order to continue game and/or action								
	2.1	Indicates desire to continue familiar game and/or action								

ACTIVITY CENTERS/FREE PLAY

Developmental level: Three to Six Years

Potential assessment areas: Fine Motor, Gross Motor, Adaptive, Cognitive, Social-Communication, Social

Materials:

Art Center: paper, crayons, pencils, scissors, posters on wall with shapes, objects, and letters

Dress-Up Center: coats, hats, shoes, pants, shirts, socks

Manipulative Center: puzzles, blocks, Tinkertoys, Legos, Lincoln Logs

Outdoor Center: bicycles, balls, playground equipment

STEP 1

MORNING ROUTINE

As the children arrive in the classroom, observe each child's ability to greet others.

Area and strand		Goals/objectives	Children's initials							
			S	N	S	N	S	N	S	N
Soc A	1.4	Initiates greetings to others who are familiar								

STEP 2

ART CENTER

Model writing and drawing. Watch the children for demonstration of these skills. Use posters on the wall as examples of shapes, objects, and letters for the children to copy. Model drawing and writing letters as needed. Provide child-size scissors and paper. Model cutting across paper, cutting along a line, and cutting out shapes as needed.

Area and strand		Goals/objectives	Children's initials							
			S	N	S	N	S	N	S	N
FM B	G1	Writes using three-finger grasp								
	1.1	Uses three-finger grasp to hold writing implement								
	G2	Prints pseudo-letters								

Area and strand		Goals/objectives	Children's initials							
			S	N	S	N	S	N	S	N
FM B	2.1	Draws using representational figures								
	2.2	Copies complex shapes								
	2.3	Copies simple shapes								
	G3	Prints first name								
	3.1	Prints three letters								
	3.2	Copies first name								
	3.3	Copies three letters								
FM A	G2	Cuts out shapes with curved lines								
	2.1	Cuts out shapes with straight lines								
	2.2	Cuts paper in two								

MANIPULATIVE CENTER

STEP 3

Observe each child's ability to handle blocks, to put puzzles together, and to assemble Tinkertoys, Lincoln Logs, or Legos.

Area and strand		Goals/objectives	Children's initials							
			S	N	S	N	S	N	S	N
FM A	G1	Uses two hands to manipulate objects, each hand performing different movements								
	1.1	Holds object with one hand while the other hand manipulates								

DRESS-UP CENTER

STEP 4

Observe each child's ability to dress and undress. As the children are playing with the dress-up clothing, observe their demonstrations of imaginary play skills (e.g., a child puts on a hat and high heels and pretends to be Mommy going shopping; a child says, "I'm going to ride my motorcycle," holding her hands in front of her and making "motor" noises).

Area and strand		Goals/objectives	Children's initials							
			S	N	S	N	S	N	S	N
Adap C	G1	Unfastens fasteners on garments								
	1.1	Unfastens buttons/snaps/Velcro fasteners on garments								
	1.2	Unties string-type fastener								
	1.3	Unzips zipper								
	2.1	Puts on long pants								
	2.2	Puts on front-opening garment								
	2.3	Puts on pullover garment								
	2.4	Puts on shoes								
	2.5	Puts on underpants, shorts, or skirt								
	G3	Fastens fasteners on garments								
	3.1	Ties string-type fastener								
	3.2	Fastens buttons/snaps/Velcro fasteners								
	3.3	Threads and zips zipper								
Cog F	G1	Engages in cooperative, imaginary play								
	1.1	Enacts roles or identities								
	1.2	Plans and acts out recognizable event, theme, or storyline								
	1.3	Uses imaginary props								

STEP 5

OUTSIDE

As children move and play around the building or playground, watch for demonstration of gross motor skills. As the children participate in organized games outside, observe their participation skills (e.g., several children play Tag or Follow the Leader). While the children are involved in activities outside, watch for them to look for and respond to peers.

Area and strand		Goals/objectives	Children's initials							
			S	N	S	N	S	N	S	N
GM A	G1	Runs avoiding obstacles								
	G2	Alternates feet walking up and down stairs								
	2.1	Walks up and down stairs								
GM B	G1	Jumps forward								
	1.1	Jumps in place								
	1.2	Jumps from platform								
	1.3	Balances on one foot								
	G2	Bounces, catches, kicks, and throws ball								
	2.1	Bounces ball								
	2.2	Catches ball								
	2.3	Kicks ball								
	2.4	Throws ball								
	G3	Skips								
	3.1	Hops								
	G4	Rides and steers two-wheel bicycle								
	4.1	Pedals and steers two-wheel bicycle with training wheels								
Cog F	G2	Engages in games with rules								
	2.1	Maintains participation								
	2.2	Conforms to game rules								
Soc A	G1	Interacts with others as play partners								
	1.1	Responds to others in distress or need								
	1.2	Establishes and maintains proximity to others								
	1.3	Takes turns with others								
	1.4	Initiates greetings to others who are familiar								

Area and strand		Goals/objectives	Children's initials							
			S	N	S	N	S	N	S	N
Soc A	1.5	Responds to affective initiations from others								

TOILETING/WASHING

STEP 6

Observe whether child demonstrates personal hygiene and undressing skills.

Area and strand		Goals/objectives	Children's initials							
			S	N	S	N	S	N	S	N
Adap B	G1	Carries out all toileting functions								
	1.1	Uses toilet paper, flushes toilet, washes hands after using toilet								
	1.2	Uses toilet								
	1.3	Indicates need to use toilet								
Adap C	2.5	Puts on underpants, shorts, or skirt								
	G3	Fastens fasteners on garments								

THROUGHOUT THE DAY

STEP 7

When the children are washing up after a messy activity and before or after snack time, watch for demonstration of grooming skills as appropriate. As the children are given choices in activities or objects, watch for the children to make choices appropriately. During activities throughout the day, observe each child's ability to resolve conflicts that arise (e.g., when a peer says that she wants a child's toys, the child says, "You can play with this one," handing the peer one of the toys). Observe the children's ability to meet their physical needs appropriately (e.g., a child asks to get a tissue for her nose or tells an adult, "I'm hungry"). As the children play independently, watch for each child's interaction skills with peers (e.g., a child asks a peer to play with her, or a child hands a peer some toys).

At the end of the unstructured play periods, observe each child's ability to follow classroom rules such as cleaning up, moving to other activities, preparing for snack time or outdoor activities, toileting, and getting ready to go home at the end of the day. Also watch for each child's ability to follow directions during these times. Observe each child's ability to participate appropriately in small and large group activi-

ties. *Observe the children for demonstration of communication skills. Unstructured play times and transition times are often good opportunities for taking language samples in order to score Social-Communication Strand B. At the end of activities or the class session, observe each child's ability to describe a story or classroom events to a naive listener (e.g., a parent).*

Area and strand		Goals/objectives	Children's initials							
			S	N	S	N	S	N	S	N
Adap B	G2	Washes and grooms self								
	2.1	Uses tissue to clean nose								
	2.2	Brushes teeth								
	2.4	Brushes or combs hair								
	2.5	Washes and dries face								
Soc A	G1	Interacts with others as play partners								
	G2	Initiates cooperative activity								
	2.1	Joins others in cooperative activity								
	2.2	Maintains cooperative participation with others								
	2.3	Shares or exchanges objects								
	G3	Resolves conflicts by selecting effective strategy								
	3.1	Negotiates to resolve conflicts								
	3.2	Uses simple strategies to resolve conflicts								
	3.3	Claims and defends possessions								
Soc B	G1	Initiates and completes age-appropriate activities								
	1.1	Responds to request to finish activity								
	1.2	Responds to request to begin activity								
	G2	Watches, listens, and participates during small group activities								
	2.1	Interacts appropriately with materials during small group activities								

Area and strand		Goals/objectives	Children's initials							
			S	N	S	N	S	N	S	N
Soc B	2.2	Responds appropriately to directions during small group activities								
	2.3	Looks at appropriate object, person, or event during small group activities								
	2.4	Remains with group during small group activities								
	G3	Watches, listens, and participates during large group activities								
	3.1	Interacts appropriately with materials during large group activities								
	3.2	Responds appropriately to directions during large group activities								
	3.3	Looks at appropriate object, person, or event during large group activities								
	3.4	Remains with group during large group activities								
Soc C	G1	Meets physical needs in socially appropriate ways								
	1.1	Meets physical needs when uncomfortable, sick, hurt, or tired								
	1.2	Meets observable physical needs								
	1.3	Meets physical needs of hunger and thirst								
	2.2	Follows established rules at home and in classroom								
Soc D	G1	Communicates personal likes and dislikes								
	1.1	Initiates preferred activities								
	1.2	Selects activities and/or objects								

Area and strand		Goals/objectives	Children's initials							
			S	N	S	N	S	N	S	N
Cog C	G1	Follows directions of three or more related steps that are not routinely given								
	1.1	Follows directions of three or more related steps that are routinely given								
	G3	Retells event in sequence								
	3.1	Completes sequence of familiar story or event								
SC A	G2	Uses conversational rules								
	2.1	Alternates between speaker/listener role								
	2.2	Responds to topic changes initiated by others								
	2.3	Asks questions for clarification								
	2.4	Responds to contingent questions								
	2.5	Initiates context-relevant topics								
	2.6	Responds to others' topic initiations								

OBSTACLE COURSE

Developmental level: Three to Six Years

Potential assessment areas: Fine Motor, Gross Motor, Adaptive, Cognitive, Social-Communication, Social

Materials: Bicycles, balance beam, jump rope, balls, playground equipment, stairs, string, tape

Children bring from home: T-shirts, shorts, athletic shoes, socks

STEP 1

For this activity, tell the children that they will be following an obstacle course and doing exercises. Give children directions involving three steps (e.g., "Take off your school shoes, put them on the bench, and then put on your tennies"; "Go to the bathroom, put on your shorts, and then line up by the door"). If the children are asked to change their clothes, then observe each child's ability to unfasten buttons/snaps/Velcro fasteners on garments, to untie string fasteners, and to open zippers. Watch for fine motor skills as the children put on their exercise clothing. As the children dress, watch for them to demonstrate adaptive skills.

Area and strand		Goals/objectives	Children's initials							
			S	N	S	N	S	N	S	N
Cog C	1.1	Follows directions of three or more related steps that are routinely given								
Adap C	G1	Unfastens fasteners on garments								
	1.1	Unfastens buttons/snaps/Velcro fasteners on garments								
	1.2	Unties string-type fastener								
	1.3	Unzips zipper								
	2.3	Puts on pullover garment								
	2.4	Puts on shoes								
	2.5	Puts on underpants, shorts, or skirt								
	G3	Fastens fasteners on garments								
	3.1	Ties string-type fastener								

Area and strand		Goals/objectives	Children's initials							
			S	N	S	N	S	N	S	N
Adap C	3.2	Fastens buttons/snaps/Velcro fasteners								
	3.3	Threads and zips zipper								

When the children are dressed, give directions using spatial concepts to tell them to put their clothes away and to get into a line (e.g., "Put your shoes on the shelf," "Put your socks in your shoes," "Stand behind the line," "Line up in front of the swings"). Have an adult lead the children through the obstacle course the first time through. Model walking up and down stairs. Observe the children using the equipment. Encourage them to stand on one foot, jump in place, jump from a platform, and jump over a jump rope placed on the ground. Observe each child's ability to run through an open area of the course and around obstacles in another part. Later, encourage the children to hop and then skip through the course. Allow the children to ride bicycles through another portion of the course. Encourage the children to stand in a circle in a clear area. Give each pair of children a ball. Encourage the children to bounce, throw, catch, and kick their balls.

Area and strand		Goals/objectives	Children's initials							
			S	N	S	N	S	N	S	N
Cog A	3.1	Demonstrates understanding of 12 different spatial relations concepts								
GM A	G1	Runs avoiding obstacles								
	1.1	Runs								
	G2	Alternates feet walking up and down stairs								
	2.1	Walks up and down stairs								
GM B	G1	Jumps forward								
	1.1	Jumps in place								
	1.2	Jumps from platform								
	1.3	Balances on one foot								
	G2	Bounces, catches, kicks, and throws ball								

Area and strand		Goals/objectives	Children's initials							
			S	N	S	N	S	N	S	N
GM B	2.1	Bounces ball								
	2.2	Catches ball								
	2.3	Kicks ball								
	2.4	Throws ball								
	G3	Skips								
	3.1	Hops								
	G4	Rides and steers two-wheel bicycle								
	4.1	Pedals and steers two-wheel bicycle with training wheels								

STEP 3

After the first time through the course, have the children take turns being the leader and giving instructions. Watch for social interactions between children. Throughout the activity, observe the children for demonstration of large group participation skills. Allow the children to play independently with the obstacle course materials toward the end of the activity. This will provide additional opportunities to observe target behaviors.

Area and strand		Goals/objectives	Children's initials							
			S	N	S	N	S	N	S	N
SC A	1.5	Uses words, phrases, or sentences to make commands to and requests of others								
	1.6	Uses words, phrases, or sentences to obtain information								
	1.7	Uses words, phrases, or sentences to inform								
Soc A	G1	Interacts with others as play partners								
	1.1	Responds to others in distress or need								
	1.2	Establishes and maintains proximity to others								

Area and strand		Goals/objectives	Children's initials							
			S	N	S	N	S	N	S	N
Soc B	G3	Watches, listens, and participates during large group activities								
	3.1	Interacts appropriately with materials during large group activities								
	3.2	Responds appropriately to directions during large group activities								
	3.3	Looks at appropriate object, person, or event during large group activities								
	3.4	Remains with group during large group activities								

STEP 4

To end the activity, give three-step directions to instruct the children to take off their exercise clothing and to put on their street clothes or to make the transition to the next activity (e.g., "Go to the bathroom, change clothes, and wash your hands for snack"). If the children are wearing gym clothes, then watch for fine motor skills as they change into their street clothing. Also observe self-care skills as the children are changing. When the children have finished dressing, use three-step directions to tell them to put their clothes away (e.g., "Put your shoes and shorts in your bag, put your bag in your cubby, and sit down for snack").

Area and strand		Goals/objectives	Children's initials							
			S	N	S	N	S	N	S	N
Cog C	1.1	Follows directions of three or more related steps that are routinely given								
Adap C	G1	Unfastens fasteners on garments								
	1.1	Unfastens buttons/snaps/Velcro fasteners on garments								
	1.2	Unties string-type fastener								
	1.3	Unzips zipper								

Area and strand		Goals/objectives	Children's initials							
			S	N	S	N	S	N	S	N
Adap C	G3	Fastens fasteners on garments								
	3.1	Ties string-type fastener								
	3.2	Fastens buttons/snaps/Velcro fasteners								
	3.3	Threads and zips zipper								

PLAYDOUGH

Developmental level: Three to Six Years

Potential assessment areas: Fine Motor, Gross Motor, Cognitive, Social-Communication, Social

Materials: Playdough (various colors); rollers, forks, spoons, cookie cutters placed in containers with lids (at least four); pieces of screen; toothbrushes

STEP 1

Introduce the activity by asking each child to choose a canister of cookie cutters. Allow children to choose playdough and any other objects that they would like to work with. One child may be put "in charge" of a specific color or toy. Encourage the children to identify items by color or shape. See if children are able to use problem-solving skills to open their containers. Make balls of playdough and model counting them. Observe children's ability to count. Ask children who do not imitate this action how many pieces of playdough they have.

Area and strand		Goals/objectives	Children's initials							
			S	N	S	N	S	N	S	N
Soc B	1.2	Responds to request to begin activity								
Soc D	G1	Communicates personal likes and dislikes								
	1.2	Selects activities and/or objects								
Cog A	1.1	Demonstrates understanding of eight different colors								
	1.2	Demonstrates understanding of five different shapes								
Cog E	G1	Evaluates solutions to problems								
	1.1	Suggests acceptable solutions to problems								
	1.2	Identifies means to goal								
Cog G	G1	Counts at least 20 objects								
	1.1	Counts at least 10 objects								
	1.2	Counts three objects								

Allow the children to play independently with the playdough. Observe them for demonstration of fine motor skills.

Area and strand		Goals/objectives	Children's initials							
			S	N	S	N	S	N	S	N
FM A	G1	Uses two hands to manipulate objects, each hand performing different movements								
	1.1	Holds object with one hand while the other hand manipulates								

Watch for each child to initiate, join, and maintain participation with others (e.g., children ask each other for different cookie cutters or for a piece of playdough of a particular color; a child offers to trade a roller for a toothbrush). Observe children's ability to resolve their own conflicts.

Area and strand		Goals/objectives	Children's initials							
			S	N	S	N	S	N	S	N
Soc A	G2	Initiates cooperative activity								
	2.1	Joins others in cooperative activity								
	2.2	Maintains cooperative participation with others								
	2.3	Shares or exchanges objects								
	G3	Resolves conflicts by selecting effective strategy								
	3.1	Negotiates to resolve conflicts								
	3.2	Uses simple strategies to resolve conflicts								
	3.3	Claims and defends possessions								

Give the children instructions to follow that involve several steps. Have the children take turns giving each other instructions, too (e.g., "Put the cookie cutter on the table; take a fork and push it into your cookie"). While giving instructions, use color, shape, size, qualitative, quantitative, spatial, and temporal concepts. Watch for children to demonstrate skills involving small-group participation.

Area and strand		Goals/objectives	Children's initials							
			S	N	S	N	S	N	S	N
Cog A	1.1	Demonstrates understanding of eight different colors								
	1.2	Demonstrates understanding of five different shapes								
	1.3	Demonstrates understanding of six different size concepts								
	2.1	Demonstrates understanding of 10 different qualitative concepts								
	2.2	Demonstrates understanding of eight different quantitative concepts								
	3.1	Demonstrates understanding of 12 different spatial relations concepts								
	3.2	Demonstrates understanding of seven different temporal relations concepts								
Cog C	G1	Follows directions of three or more related steps that are not routinely given								
	1.1	Follows directions of three or more related steps that are routinely given								
Soc B	G2	Watches, listens, and participates during small group activities								
	2.1	Interacts appropriately with materials during small group activities								
	2.2	Responds appropriately to directions during small group activities								
	2.3	Looks at appropriate object, person, or event during small group activities								
	2.4	Remains with group during small group activities								

STEP 5

To end the activity, have the children sort the materials on the basis of physical attribute (e.g., "Put the playdough into the container with a lid of the same color," and demonstrate with pieces of playdough). Have a container for each of three groups, but not for a fourth, to elicit communication. As the children are putting the materials away, encourage them to count the cookie cutters. Observe each child's ability to follow the typical routine for cleaning up after an activity.

Area and strand		Goals/objectives	Children's initials							
			S	N	S	N	S	N	S	N
Cog B	1.3	Groups objects on the basis of physical attribute								
Cog G	G1	Counts at least 20 objects								
	1.1	Counts at least 10 objects								
	1.2	Counts three objects								
SC A	G1	Uses words, phrases, or sentences to inform, direct, ask questions, and express anticipation, imagination, affect, and emotions								
	1.1	Uses words, phrases, or sentences to express anticipated outcomes								
	1.2	Uses words, phrases, or sentences to describe pretend objects, events, or people								
	1.3	Uses words, phrases, or sentences to label own or others' affect/emotions								
	1.4	Uses words, phrases, or sentences to describe past events								
	1.5	Uses words, phrases, or sentences to make commands to and requests of others								
	1.6	Uses words, phrases, or sentences to obtain information								
	1.7	Uses words, phrases, or sentences to inform								
Soc C	2.2	Follows established rules at home and in classroom								

POST OFFICE

Developmental level: Three to Six Years

Potential assessment areas: Fine Motor, Cognitive, Social-Communication, Social

Materials: Mail carrier's hat, mail bag, mailbox, rubber stamps, pencils, tape, various colors and sizes of paper, various sizes of envelopes, markers, scissors, toy money, cards with letters of the alphabet printed on them, cards with children's names printed on them

STEP 1 *Introduce the activity by describing the sequence of events for sending a letter (i.e., "First, we write a letter and put it in the envelope. Then, we write an address on the envelope and put a stamp on it. Last, we put it in the mailbox"). Ask the children to name the steps. Tell the children that they will follow these steps to send letters to friends and family members. Observe the children's ability to follow directions.*

Area and strand		Goals/objectives	Children's initials							
			S	N	S	N	S	N	S	N
Soc B	1.2	Responds to request to begin activity								
	G2	Watches, listens, and participates during small group activities								
Cog C	G1	Follows directions of three or more related steps that are not routinely given								
	G3	Retells event in sequence								

STEP 2 *Encourage the children to cut out cards and stamps to use for the activity, identifying various shapes, sizes, and colors (i.e., ask the children what colors of paper they want, which shapes they would like to cut out, what size paper they would like). Observe the children's abilities to problem-solve with tape, scissors, and limited supplies.*

Area and strand		Goals/objectives	Children's initials							
			S	N	S	N	S	N	S	N
FM A	G1	Uses two hands to manipulate objects, each hand performing different movements								
	1.1	Holds object with one hand while the other hand manipulates								
	G2	Cuts out shapes with curved lines								
	2.1	Cuts out shapes with straight lines								
	2.2	Cuts paper in two								
Cog A	1.1	Demonstrates understanding of eight different colors								
	1.2	Demonstrates understanding of five different shapes								
	1.3	Demonstrates understanding of six different size concepts								
Cog E	G1	Evaluates solutions to problems								
	1.1	Suggests acceptable solutions to problems								

STEP 3 As the children are cutting, ask them when their birthdays are so they can decide when they should send birthday cards to people in the class. During this discussion, have the children state how old they are. Then, ask the children to name people in their families and their gender. Ask them to tell if any of their family members have birthdays coming up.

Area and strand		Goals/objectives	Children's initials							
			S	N	S	N	S	N	S	N
Soc D	G3	Relates identifying information about self and others								
	3.3	States birthday								
	3.4	Names siblings and gives full name of self								
	3.5	States gender of self and others								
	3.6	States name and age								

Present children with cards with printed letters of the alphabet on them. Have the children select or identify the letters to write their names. The children can then write cards and draw pictures for other children or for family members. When the children have finished writing or coloring, ask them to select an envelope from a selection of various sizes. Ask each child for his or her name and address to write on the envelope (also ask the child for his or her telephone number).

STEP 4

Area and strand		Goals/objectives	Children's initials							
			S	N	S	N	S	N	S	N
Cog H	G3	Reads words by sight								
	3.1	Identifies letter names								
Cog A	1.3	Demonstrates understanding of six different size concepts								
Soc D	3.1	States address								
	3.2	States telephone numbers								
	3.4	Names siblings and gives full name of self								
	3.6	States name and age								

Have each child print the name and address of the letter's recipient on the envelope. (The child may need a printed model to copy from.)

STEP 5

Area and strand		Goals/objectives	Children's initials							
			S	N	S	N	S	N	S	N
FM B	G1	Writes using three-finger grasp								
	1.1	Uses three-finger grasp to hold writing implement								
	G2	Prints pseudo-letters								
	2.2	Copies complex shapes								
	2.3	Copies simple shapes								
	G3	Prints first name								
	3.1	Prints three letters								
	3.2	Copies first name								
	3.3	Copies three letters								

STEP
6

Once the letters are ready, let the children dramatize a post office situation. The children can take turns being customers and postal workers. The customers can buy stamps and mail letters; the workers talk to the customers and sell stamps. The children can identify names and letters on the envelopes, collect the mail, and deliver the mail to the children's boxes or cubbies. When the children have finished mailing and delivering the letters, have the children name the steps they performed to do so.

Area and strand		Goals/objectives	Children's initials							
			S	N	S	N	S	N	S	N
Soc B	G1	Initiates and completes age-appropriate activities								
	1.1	Responds to request to finish activity								
Cog F	G1	Engages in cooperative, imaginary play								
	1.1	Enacts roles or identities								
	1.2	Plans and acts out recognizable event, theme, or storyline								
	1.3	Uses imaginary props								
SC A	G2	Uses conversational rules								
	2.1	Alternates between speaker/listener role								
	2.2	Responds to topic changes initiated by others								
	2.3	Asks questions for clarification								
	2.4	Responds to contingent questions								
	2.5	Initiates context-relevant topics								
	2.6	Responds to others' topic initiations								
Soc A	G2	Initiates cooperative activity								
	2.1	Joins others in cooperative activity								
	2.2	Maintains cooperative participation with others								
	2.3	Shares or exchanges objects								
Cog H	G3	Reads words by sight								
	3.1	Identifies letter names								
Cog D	1.1	Recalls events that occurred on same day, with contextual cues								

STORY

Developmental level: Three to Six Years

Potential assessment areas: Cognitive, Social

Materials: Books and pillows

Have several books available for the children to choose from. Allow the children to look at or read the books. Observe each child's ability to demonstrate book-related skills. Ask each child to identify sounds and letters, use rhyming skills, blend sounds and syllables into words, segment sentences and words, sound out printed words, and read words by sight. Observe the children's ability to use reasoning skills. If necessary, ask questions to elicit these skills (e.g., "Why is the dog barking?" "What will the little pigs do if the wolf comes?").

Area and strand		Goals/objectives	Children's initials							
			S	N	S	N	S	N	S	N
Soc D	1.2	Selects activities and/or objects								
Cog H	1.1	Uses rhyming skills								
	1.2	Segments sentences and words								
	1.3	Blends single sounds and syllables								
	1.4	Identifies same and different sounds at the beginning and end of words								
	G2	Uses letter–sound associations to sound out and write words								
	2.2	Sounds out words								
	2.3	Produces correct sounds for letters								
	G3	Reads words by sight								
	3.1	Identifies letter names								
Cog E	G2	Makes statements and appropriately answers questions that require reasoning about objects, situations, or people								

		Goals/objectives	Children's initials							
Area and strand			**S**	**N**	**S**	**N**	**S**	**N**	**S**	**N**
Cog E	2.1	Gives reason for inference								
	2.2	Makes prediction about future or hypothetical events								

STEP 2

As the children look at their books, ask them to identify colors, shapes, sizes, and quality and quantity concepts, as well as spatial and temporal relations concepts (e.g., "What color is the ball?" "Show me the biggest cat," "How many ducks do you see?" "This picture has a moon and stars. Is it morning or night?"). After the children have finished looking at their books, encourage each of them to tell what their book was about. Next, read a book containing rhymes to the children and watch for their ability to participate in storytelling. Observe their ability to think of words that rhyme with words in the book (e.g., "Mat and hat rhyme with cat. What else rhymes with cat?").

		Goals/objectives	Children's initials							
Area and strand			**S**	**N**	**S**	**N**	**S**	**N**	**S**	**N**
Cog A	1.1	Demonstrates understanding of eight different colors								
	1.2	Demonstrates understanding of five different shapes								
	1.3	Demonstrates understanding of six different size concepts								
	2.1	Demonstrates understanding of 10 different qualitative concepts								
	2.2	Demonstrates understanding of eight different quantitative concepts								
	3.1	Demonstrates understanding of 12 different spatial relations concepts								
	3.2	Demonstrates understanding of seven different temporal relations concepts								
Cog C	G3	Retells event in sequence								

Area and strand		Goals/objectives	Children's initials							
			S	N	S	N	S	N	S	N
Cog C	3.1	Completes sequence of familiar story or event								
Cog E	2.3	Gives possible cause for some event								
Cog H	1.2	Segments sentences and words								

STEP 3

Throughout the activity, observe each child's ability to watch, listen, and participate during a small-group activity (i.e., Does the child remain with the group? Does he or she continue looking at books or go get a doll? Does he or she attend to the storyteller?). Encourage the children to put their books away when the activity is finished.

Area and strand		Goals/objectives	Children's initials							
			S	N	S	N	S	N	S	N
Soc B	G2	Watches, listens, and participates during small group activities								
	2.1	Interacts appropriately with materials during small group activities								
	2.2	Responds appropriately to directions during small group activities								
	2.3	Looks at appropriate object, person, or event during small group activities								
	2.4	Remains with group during small group activities								
Soc C	2.2	Follows established rules at home and in classroom								

INDEX

Page references followed by *f, t,* or *n* indicate figures, tables, or notes, respectively.

Real Progress for Every Child

As an AEPS® user, you've seen first-hand how this assessment, intervention, and programming system helps children from birth to 6 years make meaningful, measurable progress. We've taken this highly regarded tool to the next level of convenience and functionality with the exciting **web-based management system, AEPSinteractive™ (AEPSi™)!**

AEPSi™ offers the powerful reporting functions and data management help you've been looking for. With this web-based system, you can report OSEP child outcomes with the click of a button; assess multiple children simultaneously; corroborate or determine eligibility with the new cutoff scores; track child progress more effectively; easily score, aggregate, and archive AEPS® Test results; and so much more.

To learn more about how AEPSi™ can help you improve child outcomes and save time, you can

- **Register for a FREE 30-day trial.** See how AEPSi™ can work for you! Get a month of hands-on practice with AEPSi™, and discover how easy it is to create child records, prepare OSEP data, generate reports in seconds, and conduct group assessments. Sign up today at www.aepsinteractive.com.

- **Sign up for FREE webinars.** Refer to the website for information about our upcoming web-based seminars on critical topics that affect your daily work and how AEPSi™ can help.

- **Bookmark www.aepsinteractive.com.** Keep visiting this always-expanding website for the latest AEPS® news, updates, and special features.

AEPSi™. . .Real Progress for *Every* Child!

ORDERING INFORMATION

Programs new to AEPS® should plan to purchase:

- annual subscriptions to AEPSinteractive™ (AEPSi™)
- copies of the Administration Guide, Test, and Curriculum for each professional who will use the system
- training on the AEPS® system

Place your order by:

PHONE 1-800-638-3775 (toll-free)
FAX 410-337-8539
ONLINE www.aepsinteractive.com
(secure server)

AEPSinteractive™

The subscription is billed annually at the following rate
(for more details, contact an AEPS® Sales Specialist at 1-800-638-3775):

1–25 children at US$19.95 per child record per year

26–100 children at US$18.95 per child record per year

101–250 children at US$17.95 per child record per year

251–500 children at US$15.95 per child record per year

501 or more children: call Brookes Publishing for a subscription model that meets your needs

Save on Print Volume Sets

4-Volume Set
(Administration Guide, Test, both Curricula)
US$239.00 | Stock Number: 65614 • ISBN 978-1-55766-561-4

Birth to Three Set
(Administration Guide, Test, Curriculum for Birth to Three Years)
US$179.00 | Stock Number: 66024 • ISBN 978-1-55766-602-4

Three to Six Set
(Administration Guide, Test, Curriculum for Three to Six Years)
US$179.00 | Stock Number: 66031 • ISBN 978-1-55766-603-1

> **SAVE 10% ON PRINT VOLUMES WHEN YOU BUY AN AEPSi™ SUBSCRIPTION!**
> See www.aepsinteractive.com for other subscribers' benefits, including free tech support, webcasts, and OSEP Child Outcomes reports.

Sold Separately

Print Volumes
Volume 1: Administration Guide
US$65.00 | Stock Number: 65621
2002 • 336 pages • 7 x 10 • spiral-bound • ISBN 978-1-55766-562-1

Volume 2: Test: Birth to Three Years and Three to Six Years
US$75.00 | Stock Number: 65638
2002 • 304 pages • 7 x 10 • spiral-bound • ISBN 978-1-55766-563-8

Volume 3: Curriculum for Birth to Three Years
US$65.00 | Stock Number: 65645
2002 • 512 pages • 7 x 10 • spiral-bound • ISBN 978-1-55766-564-5

Volume 4: Curriculum for Three to Six Years
US$65.00 | Stock Number: 65652
2002 • 352 pages • 7 x 10 • spiral-bound • ISBN 978-1-55766-565-2

Forms on CD-ROM (PC and Mac compatible; 8.5 x 11 pdfs)
English
US$249.95 | Stock Number: 66352 • ISBN 978-1-55766-635-2

Spanish
US$199.95 • Stock Number: 68127 • ISBN 978-1-55766-812-7

Forms also sold separately in paper format; see www.aepsinteractive.com.

> **SAVE 20%**
> on the CD-ROM when you buy any AEPS set!